Global Health and Sustainable Development Architecture

Inclusive Dialogue, Partnerships, and Community Capital

Mei-Ling Wang

University Press of America,® Inc.
Lanham · Boulder · New York · Toronto · Plymouth, UK

Copyright © 2009 by
University Press of America,® Inc.
4501 Forbes Boulevard
Suite 200
Lanham, Maryland 20706
UPA Acquisitions Department (301) 459-3366

Estover Road
Plymouth PL6 7PY
United Kingdom

Library of Congress Control Number: 2009929749
ISBN-13: 978-0-7618-4752-6 (clothbound : alk. paper)
ISBN-10: 0-7618-4752-9 (clothbound : alk. paper)
ISBN-13: 978-0-7618-4753-3 (paperback : alk. paper)
ISBN-10: 0-7618-4753-7 (paperback : alk. paper)
eISBN-13: 978-0-7618-4754-0
eISBN-10: 0-7618-4754-5

For the Indigenous People

Contents

Preface

Given the convergence of all the development problems in recent years, we are asking ourselves, "what is the solution?" These problems are now growing in their magnitude every day. They no longer affect one community or one country, but have impacted the whole world. These problems combined now pose a serious challenge to the survival of humanity.

What is the solution then? Actually, these challenges are not new. Humanity has seen and has survived worse challenges before. Recently, the increasing collaboration in global health, particularly those deriving from multi-lateral agencies and American foundations, has shown that it is possible for humanity to overcome any challenges as long as there is collective will to tackle the root causes of the challenges.

In addressing the need to tackle the root causes of global development challenges, this book makes several endeavors. First, it creates a theoretical framework of sustainable development to articulate an alternative model of conceptualizing development. Second, this writing generates a Hexagon of Inclusive Partnership Model for collaborative efforts to improve sustainable development. Third, the book applies these conceptual and operational frameworks to the analysis of the fundamental elements of sustainable development, such as food, energy, and water security. Combining the thinking in public health, social policy, social epidemiology, development sociology, public communication, and management, the book aims to highlight the importance of inclusion and community capital as the critical components in sustainable development.

This writing summarizes the experiences of the vulnerable people in the world, especially the indigenous, in the fight against social, political, economic, and health adversities.

The convergence of incessant crises, epidemics, conflicts, and disasters in recent years has sent a clear message to humanity that we are in a urgent need for a different model of development. For many years, a misguided mindset of development, the "winnership" model, has put humanity and our planet on a trajectory of tremendous peril that could seriously jeopardize the chances of survival for all species. The reality in global development is such that we need a major change in our mindset. The start of the change is to recognize that given the magnitude of challenges facing us, we have no choices but to work in inclusive partnerships in a post-ideological manner.

Mei-ling Wang, Ph.D. (University of Maryland), MPH (Harvard School of Public Health), Associate Professor
March 2009

Acknowledgements

First and foremost, I would like to thank the indigenous in the United States and Latin America, who have offered me their generous support and help. Without them, this book would not be possible. They have taught me a valuable lesson about environment, mother of the livelihood for humanity. I am humbled by the tenacity and courage that they have demonstrated in the fight against formidable challenges, including genocide. They are my inspiration for the genesis of this writing.

I am particularly grateful to my indigenous friends of "Mujeres En Accion" (MEAI) in Guatemala for allowing me to witness their exclusion situations first-hand. Felipa, director of MEAI, has single-handedly taken up the daunting task to empower the indigenous women in the aftermath of the mass killings of the indigenous in Guatemala.

I am thankful to Harvard School of Public Health to equip me with the tools to embark on this journey and open my eyes to the social determinants, which are the root causes of population health problems. In particular, I would like to thank Dr. Ichiro Kawachi and Dr. Deborah Prothrow at Harvard School of Public Health, and Dr. Joan Reede, Harvard Medical School, for teaching me to apply a social epidemiological analysis to examine population health problems

The acknowledgment section would not be complete without thanking some special individuals who have inspired my work in breaking social exclusion. I would like to thank Patrik Johansson and Aranthan Jones, III, or AJ, for being role models in my work to address development and health disparities.

I also thank Ms. McVay for her help with editing.

Most importantly, my deepest gratitude goes to my father, who has taught me to respect the wisdom of the indigenous people and to be "a good earth citizen." His words and deeds sow the seed for this project, which hopefully will be of use to others to make our development path more inclusive and healthier.

Chapter 1

Global Health and Sustainable Development Architecture: An Introduction

Financial crises, energy shortage, environmental breakdown, food insecurity, intergroup conflict and epidemics, and pandemics. . . . Humanity has never seen the convergence of so many crises as in recent years. In the face of these crises, the call for urgent action has also been increasing each day. To effectuate solutions to these challenges, many questions have been asked. What has gone wrong in the development path of humanity? What is the fundamental solution? These questions require humanity to think hard and thoroughly of what we have done wrong and how we are supposed to find a solution. The first step in resolving this quagmire is to examine our mindset in thinking about development, and then it will be clear why different thinking is in tall order before humanity is moving into a development catastrophe. Without a new framework of self-reflection and alternative thinking, the multifarious, disparate programs in global health and development will achieve limited results. The purpose of this book is to answer to such a need by first analyzing the pitfalls with the conventional development paradigm and explores an alternative model about global health and development that aims for sustainable outcomes. This new framework aims to present an interdependent and collaborative approach to resolving global development challenges.

Global Health and Development Architecture

To begin with, architecture has to do with the art, science and method of designing, arranging and constructing a building (American Heritage Dictionary of the English Language, 2008); Cambridge Dictionaries On-line, 2008). Or to put it simply, architecture specifies a plan of designing a structure for a specific goal. Conceptually, this plan involves considerations of a theory, a school of thought, or a cultural tradition used to build a structure. Ideally, this structure is designed to fit the surroundings and enhance community functions. The operationalization of this plan specifies methods of construction, parties involved in contributing the labor, materials used, the timelines, testing and delivery of the final product, and maintenance plan. In a way, the architecture involved in building a physical structure is similar to our design of the development model for humanity.

Before laying out the architecture of development, it is important to examine the relationship between global health and sustainable development.

Global health problems stem from development challenges, and therefore their solutions cannot be separate from solutions to correct misguided actions in global development. Therefore, global health architecture is encrusted in the larger global development architecture.

Population and social health plays a key role in sustainable development because it often offers the most valid indicators to gauge global development. Therefore, the starting point to lay out global health and sustainable development architecture is to elucidate the challenges facing humanity today. As mentioned earlier, there are many challenges facing humanity today, but the most daunting challenge is our failure of climbing out of our cave of habitual thinking and engaging in creative imagination. That is, we are facing barriers of development because of our failure in imagining alternative solutions to resolve pressing concerns facing the global community. Indeed, in the history of humanity, we have never faced so many threats at the same time. From global financial crises, the scourge of epidemics and pandemics, the ravaging impact of environmental disintegration and climate irregularities, to the decimating toll from wars and conflicts, we are confronted with problems, mostly of our own making.

By every measure of the health of our planet, community or individual health, humanity does not fare well. Evidence has never been more convincing to persuade even the skeptics about the seriousness of our survival challenges. On the front of population health, by 2007, more than 25 million people have died of AIDS and another 36 million are living with HIV/AIDS (AVERT, 2008). "Worldwide HIV/AIDS Statistics"). On malaria, about 500 million of people are infected by malaria every year (WHO, 2008, "Malaria"). About 500 million people are infected by malaria every year (WHO, 2008, "Malaria."). In one estimate, about 50 million people will become environmental refugees by 2010, and about 1 billion will be in this category by 2050 in the aftermath of earthquakes, hurricanes, droughts, famines, and floods (Deen, 2008). These adverse events can be attributed to global warming, climate change, desertification and land degradation, rising sea levels, deforestation, soil erosion, and crop deletion (Deen, 2008). Just the event of the Katrina hurricane caused the displacement of 1 million individuals in the United States (Deen, 2008). Iin October, 2008, in the height of the global financial crisis, it was estimated that as of October 24, 2008, global equities had lost about 27 percent of their value (Norris, 24 October 2008). Just in the United States alone, American retirement plans had lost $2 trillion in 15 months (Yahoo News, October, 2008. "Retirement accounts have lost $2 trillion so far"). And this crisis is seen as the worst since the Great Depression. Worse, these problems seem to have coalesced and have multiplied in their destructive force against humanity. Now, we are more threatened than at any point in the history by the unstable force of globalization, dwindling of natural resources, inequities and disparities of all sorts, ideological antagonism, and community breakdowns.

While we are facing the increasing challenges of natural disasters and spread of diseases, we are engrossed in an even more dangerous practice of an ideological warfare that exaggerates our differences in race/ethnicity, nation states, religions, class, gender and sexuality, etc. This war has created an even larger conflict for vulnerable populations. Globally, about 42 million people have become the victims of conflicts (PAWSS, 2008, "Refugees, forcible displacement, and international security"). And every day, we are alarmed by our deepest fear that the nuclear weapons created by our advanced technologies could be in the wrong hands and would lead to a total annihilation of humanity.

It is obvious that the root cause of the problem is not the uncontrollable force of nature but our failure to harness the strengths of humanity for the larger gains for global community and for our planet, the source of our survival. All of a sudden, humanity is struggling to re-discover our ingenious impetus that has saved humanity from extinction in our evolutionary process.

The first step in recovering our remarkable talent in solving survival challenges is self-reflection by examining the assumptions and ideologies that have not worked toward the goal of sustainable development. A number of theories in the political economy of international development that examine the ideologies of development provide a useful reference framework for the analysis of the prevailing assumptions of the conventional paradigm of development. To begin with, the study of political economy seeks to explicate the interaction between political power and economic outcomes (see Crane, 1997). It adds theoretical robustness to the discipline of political science or the study of economics by including the economic processes and structures in its analysis. The objects of its analysis include all the international actors or stakeholders in the process of development, which includes but is not limited to states, global businesses, intergovernmental agencies, civil society, communities, and so on (see Crane, 1997). There are several sets of theories in international political economy that are relevant to an explanation of the development process of the past four hundred years. To begin with, mercantilism sees state interest as the most important rationale that justifies state policies in economics. Mercantilist policies seek to maximize state power and wealth through economic policies. In contrast, liberalisim, advanced by Adam Smith and David Ricardo, believes that the pursuit of self-interest in a market system will lead to efficiency and prosperity, that is, economic development. Keynes's argument for state intervention in economic development provides a place for state policies in steering economic development. Neo-liberalism further clarifies that in the context of an interdependent world, global economic development is predicated on the pursuit of peace. Robert Keohane and Joseph Nye suggest that military power is relevant only in matters of national security interest. In addition, structuralism serves as a critical framework to explicate why the mercantilist and liberal approaches have not worked for the developing countries. Or to be precise, it has offered a robust criticism about the problems of capitalism in relation to underdevelopment in those countries. The world systems theory and underdevelopment theory explain the need for uneven economic stratification in the global capitalist system, with some in the center and others in the periphery, and this stratification then contributes to underdevelopment for the peripheral countries. Lastly, postmodernism, based on Antonio Gramsci''s original formulation, tries to explain the complex relationships among state, means of production, and social class. In another word, the capitalist mode of production has shaped the definitions of national interest, class relations, and cultural productions.

In the reference framework of these theories, the key assumption of the prevailing model of development descends from a primitive mode of human survival that sees development as a zero-sum game mainly about economic competition and nation building. That is, some will gain and others will lose. A tribe, a people, or a nation state must always maintain its advantageous positions through an "acquisitive" and "expansionist" mentality. That is, the winner constantly extends its frontiers, be they geographical, political, economic, or cultural, through aggressive means, such as visible or ideological wars. This approach sees no limits to acquisition or asserting the "winnership." Because of this mode of thinking, recent human history sees the emergence and replacement of one winner by the other, repeating the same winnership mentality that emphasizes the building of an empire. Yet this is not to deny that there are some who do not quite agree with this view of development. As mentioned earlier, the "interdependence" theorists tend to emphasize the dividend of peace in economic development and the structuralists constantly remind us the danger in the prevailing development model in enlarging the gap between the haves and have-nots both intra-nationally and internationally. For a long time, the dominant model tends to see development as predicated on the gains in material well-being and national power. However, very few have thoroughly examined the end goal of development or provided a true alternative to the current "economic competition" model.

Certainly, we could not deny that there are practical utilities in this model of development. Indeed, in the span of four hundred years, humanity has made a large number of incredible achievements, especially in science, technology, and medicine, but the fruits of these advancements have not been evenly spread to all humanity. In fact, in some cases, they have created an even large inequality. These achievements have not resolved our fundamental dilemma of lacking a more equitable solution to global development. Certain ideas espoused in these development theories of mercantilism, realism, statism, classical liberalism, and neoclassical liberalism, have contributed to this dilemma (Portes, 1997; Rapley, 2004; Harvey, 2005; and Prasad, 2006). And despite the robust theoretical power of socialism and communism, their solutions have not totally resolved the problem of competitive ethos underlying the empire-building development paradigm.

For a long time, the "winnership" model provides the dominant definition of progress and modernization and has shaped the path of the international development for about four hundred years. First of all, the prevailing paradigm is steeped in the assumption that there is a single and uniform standard of human development, and it equates economic, material growth as development. In this framework, the measure of development is based on the measure of tangible capital, as mostly reflected in concrete calculation of material achievement. A nation state would have to accumulate a certain amount of financial capital, or in today's terms, the total of GDP, to be considered as moving into the ranks of a developed state. To stimulate growth, the state often has to take actions to protect its so-called "national interests." And a government's policies are designed to support a narrowly defined objective of national interests, often for the growth of the GDP or for military prowess/global dominance. Towards this end, government has to find ways to increase its national power or sustain its dominance. One of the fastest routes is to resort to the use of wars or aggressive trade policies to accumulate financial capital and protect this financial gain through the exercise of political and military power. Trade that benefits a state's economic interest is seen as the engine of growth. When trading is favorable to a given state's economic agenda, a government uses political means to breakdown trade barriers but will strengthen protectionist mechanisms when trade is perceived as counterproductive to its nation-building objective. Since development is seen as a function of a numerical game, the widening of the gap between the haves and have-nots is often tolerated. The haves are motivated to pursue further their financial advantage. This can occur within a given nation state or in the world system. There is little interest in examining how this gigantic gap or excess capital could be reinvested to improve inequity. Fourth, in this development model, not everyone or every state has an equal access to the knowledge, networks or resources to engage in the world's prevailing financial game. Subtle, or not too subtle, boundaries are built in terms of who could be the beneficiaries of the gains and who could not. In some cases, some arbitrary criteria based on centuries-old cultural or social ideologies have been used to sustain these boundaries, such as gender, racial/ethnic affiliations, religious distinction, class/cast, or geography. This boundary-setting process creates exclusion that precludes certain populations or groups from access the financial gains. It then results in other types of socioeconomic and political disparities.

In modern times, the appearance of economic prosperity, as reflected in the glamorous GDP growth and accumulation of financial capital, hides the unsettling consequences of gigantic disparities between a very small number of the haves and the majority of the have-nots. To gain more, the haves have to continue to maximize financial returns through aggressive investments, often at the expense of the have-nots. The momentum of the capital flow is such that it often moves toward those who already have distinct advantages in the financial game, while the majority of individuals often lose out in this financial game. It creates a situation of financial stratification that deepens inequity or exclusion. In this sense, social exclusion is the inevitable by-product of the empire building approach.

Evidence of exclusionary practices abounds in history. Slavery was the most relevant case in point (See Genovese, 1967). The adroit use of arbitrary inter-group differences to justify the distribution of economic gains and then political hierarchy, underlain the success of the strong states in the modern times. The mercantilist ambition led to aggressive colonization in Africa, Asia, and the Americas for the exploitation of natural resources and slavery for the purpose of building the strong states at home. The gains from colonization have paved the way for economic prosperity, political dominance, and to certain extent religious dominance from these "strong states." For example, the exploitation in Africa sustained the industrial revolution in Europe (Twells and Smith, 1992). The use of slavery to maximize the profits of cotton, sugar, and tobacco by the early settlers paved the economic foundation of the United States (Genovese, 1961) The colonial game reflected certain exclusionary criteria. Racial superiority ideology, as advanced in Rudyard Kipling's poem "The White Man's Burden" was used to justify colonialism in Africa. (Jordan, 1974). The idea that the goal of economic prowess determines social and political organizations becomes the norm, the gold standard of development.

The other example is the socioeconomic equities associated with gender. Throughout human history, the perceived biological vulnerabilities of women have been perceived as weaker capacities and have been used to justify their lesser share in social and economic lives (Benocraitis, 1997; Smith, Hopkins, and Muhammad, 1988). The distortion of religious texts to suit a biased gender ideology is not a new practice and has been conveniently abused to create a spiral of silence that prevents a truly rational discourse on the issue. This gender war is particularly telling in the political milieu when political candidates try to distort religious teachings to perpetuate a certain gender practice that limits the liberties of vulnerable gender groups, consisting of both men and women. Political debates have been forced to focus on the narrow debate of morality associated with different gender practices. Often, the discussion is limited to a simplistic, moral dichotomy of evil and good, such as in the cases of abortion or homosexuality, while ignoring other more relevant issues of gender relations, economic opportunities, biological differences, and public health implications.

In the development paradigm that prevailed before the Second World War, development was seen as a linear process with a predetermined model of competition for "winnership." The world was then divided into conquers vs. the conquerors; lords vs. slaves; exploiters versus the exploited; and owners vs. the deprived.

Despite the fact that after the War, the old model of development has been challenged, but this "winnership" model continues to exist in other derivative forms, such as through unfettered force of globalization in trade, financial deregulation, cultural dominance or environmental imperialism.

In this framework of thinking, the standard-setters often did not take into account the inclusion of other "intangible" capital in the measure of development. One of the examples of the intangible capital is the ecological knowledge of indigenous peoples or "minimalist" lifestyle that contributes to their harmony and protection of our environment; however, their practices have never been recognized as development.

The negative consequences of the conventional development paradigm began emerging after a series of international wars, such as the First World War, the Korean War, and the Vietnam War. And till this day, despite some efforts to correct the erroneous assumptions of the old paradigm, the negative consequences remain very serious barriers to sustainable development. To begin with, these wars were the inevitable consequences of the application of the winnership model of thinking because of the collision of course among the dominant actors in global competition. Those world wars were not really "world wars," because the major players were only a few of those strong states, those colonizers whose interests collided when the competitive game became throat-cutting and left other vulnerable groups to be the unwilling victims. The victim groups happened to be those considered as the "less developed" ethnic, religious or gender groups. The development scheme generated by the "strong states" in the post-war arrangements has not ameliorated the negative consequences of these development ideas because that dominant idea of development has not changed.

The lack of a vision and revision to change the dominant paradigm has led to even more micro- or regional conflicts. The combined damages resulting from these conflicts in terms of human lives lost have exceeded the total loss of the two World Wars. Since the end of the World War II in 1945, the world has not seen sustainable peace and development, but only heightened conflicts. The uneven development in Africa, South America, and Asia in the post colonial era has actually extended certain colonial tendencies in the form of ideological mobilization, environmental imperialism, and global financial liberalization (or unfettered free trade) and has left landmines for future explosive conflicts among the historical or ideological rivals.

The uneven development experienced in global communities could be attributed to the inability to change the centuries-old idea about what truly constitutes development. This idea leads to the uneven appropriation of global resources to different regions based on the decisions related to ideological affinities, (the struggle between communism and capitalism), race, and religious differences. The tactics of divide and rule, which had been widely used during the colonial era, were recycled again during the Cold War, Korean War, the Vietnam War, the first Afghanistan War, and the Iraq War. These wars were the manifestation of the "winnership" model among rivaling strong states. That is, despite whatever legitimate claims or righteous pretensions on the basis of which the wars were fought, they were about self-aggrandizement to achieve "winnership." Winnership supports an idea of presumed moral superiority of the winning states, who claim to uphold the only, unique and infallible standard to measure human progress, despite the practical impossibility of the existence of such a claim.

Ideological differences have become the most convenient vehicle to justify confrontation, hatred, and wars for self-gains. The strong states fought out their ideological battles not on own their own territories but on the turfs of their former colonies or the weak states serving as their surrogates in the so-called developing countries. The Vietnam War was the extension of the ideological conflict between capitalist and communist blocs. In the 1990s, the first Afghanistan War was a similar story. Under the excuse of fighting terrorism, the Iraq War could also be seen as the extension of the exaggerated rivalry of Islam and Christianity with the added motive of economic acquisition because of the fact that Iraq has one of the largest oil reserves in the world. This primitive model of development has caused damages that have far-reaching implications for global health and development. It is obvious by now that these damages are beyond immediate repair.

These damages are manifested in every aspect of global lives and their effects are not limited any more to one group of individuals, one single community, an isolated geographical area, or one dimension of communal activities. On the economic front, there emerges a "super-size culture" in economic gains and consumption. In the macro-context, the emphasis of the growth-driven model of development, has led to a fanatical pursuit of the growth of GDP or increase of personal wealth, often at the expense of the underprivileged. At the micro-level, the super-size culture has encouraged unlimited consumption. The indulgence in consumption has affected the integrity of the social system, the economy, and ecology. That is, the consumers have been encouraged, cajoled, and pushed over the limit for their desire for new products. In a scenario of limited incomes, individuals are encouraged to spend beyond their means. Inevitably, consumers are now relying on the use of credit to pre-pay things that they cannot afford at the present. The material advances, which are supposed to be a fantastic engine of development, become fantastic demons of the bridesmaid syndrome. That is, humanity is sucked into a never ending process of catching up with the products of the trends, so that we have to cash in on our future earnings to fulfill mostly artificially created needs. This process inevitably becomes a debt on our current balance sheet. The rise of the credit card debt culture in most of the industrialized or near-industrialized societies, such as in Australia, the United States, United Kingdom, Japan, Taiwan, and Hong Kong, attests to the prevalence of this culture.

The financial institutions have aggravated this culture by enticing the consumers to be addicted to payment schemes that deepen the consumers' debt dependency. This creates a vicious cycle of consumption dependency. So when consumers cannot not afford payment for the debt due to unexpected circumstances, the health of the economy suffers, as in the case of the sub-prime crisis.

Worse, the modern development model heavily depends on oil as the engine of growth. Once oil supply is threatened, global conflicts increase and economic recession sets in, as has occurred since the end of 2007. The bad habits of lacking a vision and prevention put humanity in further jeopardy. The plundering and exploitation in the past four hundred years to sustain this unsustainable growth and expansion model puts unexpected strains on our environment, the mother of our livelihood. The excessive consumption has created a culture of waste and the endless plundering of our natural environment to satisfy our insatiable consumption has endangered the natural habitat crucial for our food and water security, ecological and environmental sustainability. The endless environmental incidents and ecological disasters, such as hurricanes, earthquakes, floods, climate change, and desertization of farming soil, have directly and indirectly contributed to food crises, water shortage, and increasing spread of diseases.

The political economy of winnership, especially in political aggran-
dizements and economic expansion, has seriously affected the fundamentals of
international relations. In the scenario of dwindling resources (especially oil,
food, and water), the potential for conflicts has also increased. In other words,
we have become more barbaric in our acquisition of resources than our "barbaric" ancestors. At least, with their limited knowledge of war tools, our pre-
sumably "barbaric" ancestors did limited damage to themselves, other species,
or the environment. Today, international problems are multiplying at a faster
pace than solutions can be found because those isolated or excluded nation states
have to use even more radical means pre-empt their opponents or to advance
their own gains and since they have been excluded from international frameworks, they have very little incentive to abide by the international rules. In the
beginning of April, 2009, the nuclear missile crisis created by North Korea is
such a case in point. Acting on its radical impulses becomes North Korea's most
used tactic to advance its own agenda. At the time, North Korea was attempting
to launch a nuclear missile despite the repeated warnings from the international
community against such a move.

This case shows another problem of the old model of development, in
which the goal of the strong states is to consolidate their winnership, through
increasing allegiance or through the prevention of the rise of "alternative
power." Consolidation or expansion a lot of times is conducted at the expense
of conflict resolution. Since the end of World War II, the world has done less to
bridge differences or ameliorate conflicts than to aggravating differences. Political antagonism is fully exploited to maintain this winnership. This is also true
for other types of divisions, especially religious differences.

Groups of different beliefs have not ceased to create a virtual enemy
out of each other to perpetuate their own power. The creation of Southeast Asian
Nations (SEAN) was to counter the Soviet influence (Association of Southeast
Asian Nations. 2008, "Overview." http://www.aseansec.org/64.htm). The expansion of the EU (European Union) was at the expense of the non-EU states.
The case of EU is particularly alarming because since 2008, the expansion of
EU without Russia's full blessing has created more tensions between EU and
Russia. The action of the allegiance of the dominant actors invites reaction from
those "not in the club." Eventually, they have to create their own allegiances to
defend their interest and counter the expansion pressure of those "dominant factors." Against such a background came to the fore the Muslim fundamentalist
movement.

Excessive reaction or counter-reaction creates the risk of disrupting international stability, and in the worst case, it could lead to an apocalypse or Ar-
mageddon scenario. Today, the world lives in constant anxiety because of the
creation of a virtual enemy or a perpetuation of the witch hunt that states or
groups have created out of or against each other, because of the exaggeration of
inter-group differences. Samuel Hungtington's well-known thesis about the
clashes of civilizations as an inevitable outcome from ethnic differences in international relations epitomizes such a phenomenon (Huntington, 1998). The

focal point of his observation was the need of the world to be vigilant against the rise of Islam because of the idiosyncrasy of Islam. Huntington also argues that our vigilance should be raised against other groups who are different from the West in their political, social, and cultural thinking and ways of living. And it is not surprising that this list can be quite long. This observation has its practical value in defining the possible national security threats to the United States in the post-911 world but its application to international relations could be complicated because its assumptions are eerily reminiscent of the excuses used by the crusaders to justify their atrocities against other groups of differences.

This mentality has serious implications for international development. The magnitude of the damage is reflected in the use of the tactics by some opinion leaders in addressing global conflicts. More and more, opinion leaders are inclined to create conflicts as a way to resolve conflicts. As a result, the crises are not only worsened but become the catalyst of some other crises. The most pronounced of the recent examples is the Iraq War, initiated by President Bush and supported by Britain, Australia, Poland, and Denmark (Wikipedia, 2008). In a misleading semantic manipulation, the Iraq war was declared by Mr. Bush as a preventive war (See White House. "President's Remarks at the United Nations General Assembly." 2002) while in fact there is little difference between a preventive war and aggression.

In international law, aggression is a crime against humanity and this idea is not new. As a matter of fact, the United States was one of the strongest supporter of the Kellogg-Briand pact, or the Pact of Paris, that highlighted the illegality and immorality of aggression (Davies, 2004). All the nations who signed the pact had condemned the use of war as a policy instrument. In the wake of the Second World War, the Untied States and its allies had resorted to the Kellogg-Briand Pact to convict German Nazi leaders to a death sentence entirely on the basis of the postulate that waging a aggressive war is a crime (Davies, 2004). Later, the spirit of the Pact was reasserted in the United Nations Charter, Article 2, Clause 4. In a sense, the moral claim of the Iraq War shares some similarities to the claims of righteousness of the fascist justification of their persecution of Jewish people.

The worst part of the Iraq War is that it has fully exploited ethnic and religious antagonism and economic imperialism. The supporters of the Iraq War compared their undertaking to a "crusade" to spread democracy in the Middle East (See Lobe, 2005). The subtext of this claim betrays the hidden agenda of aggression. The bizarre marriage of the words of "preventive" and "war" could not hide the truth that the idea of "crusade" is intrinsically incompatible with the idea of "democracy," because true democracy is finding common ground among differences, while a crusade is coercion to "kill" differences.

The hidden agenda of the "oil politics" in this case further adds fuel to the fire. In a comment to Tim Russert, Cheney mentioned that Iraq has the second largest oil reserves in the world, next only to those of Saudi Arabia (See Wikipedia, "Financial Cost of the Iraq War." 2008). Given the lack of other legitimate reasons for the United States to initiate the war, the theory that the major motivation of the Iraq War was the Bush administration's design on the rich oil reserves in Iraq was widely speculated by the international community (See BBC, "Oil Firms Discuss Iraqi Stake," 12 March, 2003). The Bush administration's plan to extend the stay of US troops in Iraq beyond Bush's tenure through a bilateral treaty is even more deplorable because it is a repetition of the colonialists' design for former colonies. In 2008, the Bush administration proposed, in a "Status of Forces" agreement, to the Iraqi government the setup of permanent US bases in Iraq. In addition, Bush proposed US control over Iraqi air space up to 30,000 feet and immunity from prosecution for US troops and private military contractors. These measures are widely perceived as colonial measures that would jeopardize Iraq's sovereignty. This proposed agreement by George W. Bush is not too different from the old-time imperialism waged by the strong states against vulnerable peoples (McClathy, "US Seeking 58 Military Bases in Iraq, Shiite Law Makers Say," 2008). The tactics used to conduct the Iraq War underlie a more worrisome tendency of perpetuating the out-of-date development model and the deficit of imagination to conjure alternative solutions. The lack of ingenuity of these tactics has actually created even more negative problems in an already conflict-ridden world.

The negative implications of the Iraq War have not disappeared with the departure of the Bush administration, and they are likely to be gradually emerging to the detriment to the power and moral authority of the United States in international relations. First of all, the most dangerous message that the Iraq War has sent to the world is that United States cannot not be trusted as the ultimate arbitrator of global peace because if the standard-bearer or the rule-setter like the United States can break the rules, no other countries need to follow the rules, since the rules have not been equally applied to every player. This claim could have serious implications for nuclear noproliferation. Both Iran and North Korea, the most excluded of the excluded states, are likely to test the world's limits in this area. Second, the Iraq War has justified the position of other radical powers, especially those in the Middle East, North Korea, South America, and Asia, that the world needs a new order in international operations, which might be even less stable than the current order. Third, the lack of legitimacy for the launching of the Iraq War by the United Stats has legitimized the participation of "the war business" by other radical groups. It makes the use of force and terror an even more appealing choice for the marginalized groups or states to make their case in front of an international audience. However, the political calculation behind the Iraq War is not a new approach. It is simply an extension of the old development model, i.e., "the winner takes it all." And it has generated very negative consequences for global peace, the cornerstone of sustainable development.

We are more bewildered than ever about our seemingly hopeless ineptitude in resolving global challenges. Since the end of World War II, between 1946 and 2005, there have been 403 regional conflicts. Most of the conflicts are in Africa and Asia. Just in Africa alone, there have been 224 conflicts during the period. And in Africa, the cost of wars was $300 billion between 1990 and 2005, or about 15 percent of Africa's economy. Most of the 9.5 million refugees and 23 million displaced people lived in Africa in 2005 (United Nations Development Program. "Armed Violence in Africa: Reflections on the Costs of Crime and Conflict," 2008). On the supply side, the United States, the leading exporter of weapons, accounted for $3.8 billion, or 46 percent, of global weapon sales, followed by other strong states, such as Russia, France, Germany, and Italy (Kleppe, 2007). The destination of the weapons transfer, through sale or foreign aid, is developing countries, where weapons should be on the last items of foreign aid. In one estimate, the United States and Russia topped the world in their weapon sales to developing countries. Between 2001 and 2004, the United States made sales of $29.8 billion, or 39.9 percent, in arms agreements with developing countries, followed by Russia's $21.7 billion, or 29.1 percent of the world's total (Congressional Research Service, "CRS Report for Congress: Conventional Arms Transfer to Developing Nations." 2005). The value of arms transfer agreements between the United States and developing countries was 62.7 percent of all such arms transfer agreements between 1997 to 2004. In 2004, the total value of the arms delivered to developing countries was $22.5 billion, the highest total since 2000 (Congressional Research Service. "CRS Report for Congress: Conventional Arms Transfer to Developing Nations." 2005). In contrast, only $20 billion is needed to upgrade water supply and sanitation to meet basic needs for developing countries (United Nations, "Water: A Matter of Life and Death," 2003).

The developed countries do not fare better in the economics of wars. As of June 20, 2008, in middle of the protracted Iraq War, the United States has paid more than $529 billion for war expenses (See Wikipedia, National Priorities Project, 2008). At that time, the American people were paying $341.4 million for the Iraq War every day. And in an estimate by the Congressional Budget Office, the wars of Afghanistan and Iraq could cost American people $2.4 trillion by 2017 (Wikipedia, "Financial Cost of Iraq War," 2008). In the meantime, the world is deeply anxious about the outcomes of this current economic contraction because of the convergence of several economic challenges, including the sub-prime crisis and its fallout, high unemployment, loss of economic competitiveness, and increasing natural disasters.

In this competition for winnership to carve out spheres of influence in the resource-poor, vulnerable states by feeding into centuries-old rivalry, it is no wonder that the world only sees alarming crises at much closer intervals. In Asia, the conflicts or the potential conflicts spread from East China Sea to the border of India and Pakistan. In South America, the border conflicts have created tensions among Columbia and Ecuador and Venezuela. The class war between the haves and have-nots occurs almost daily in Latin America. In Africa, the wars of small or large scale spread from the south of the continent, such as in Zimbabwe, to the north, in Sudan. Lacking innovative solutions, the incendiary rhetoric and bellicose actions used by the strong states have only inflamed an already combustible situation. The calls for human rights for the victims sound emptier than ever because they have not been applied evenly to every case of violation and are mainly used as a political weapon to counter selective international rivals.

The political, social, and economic damages brought about by the competition-driven development model have spilled over into other spheres of social lives and have seriously affected the health of humanity. Globally, the poverty level is alarming. About half of world's populations live under $2 a day (See Global Issues, 2008, "Poverty Facts and Stats'). Wealth disparity is increasing in almost every country. The richest 20 percent of the world's population accounts for 75 percent of the world's wealth (Ibid.). The poorest 40 percent account for only 5 percent of the global wealth share. And the combined wealth of the 7 richest people on earth is equivalent to the total GDP of 40 mostly indebted nations (World Bank, 2008, "Key Development Data and Statistics"). The wealth disparity between the rich countries and poor states has grown wider and wider every decade and has seriously affected social equilibrium. In one analysis, the distance between the rich states and poor states was 3 to 1 in 1820; 11 to 1 in 1913; 35 to 1 in 1950; 44 to 1 in 1973; 72 to 1 in 1972; and we see no shortening of this distance due to the exponential growth of debt of poor countries (United Nations Development Program, 1999, "Human Development Program 1999"). And it is hard to imagine how the heavily indebted countries can ever climb out of their debt cycles owed to the banks of developed countries. The old form of colonialism has transformed into a new indebted bondage. For example, in 2006, the world provided the poor states $106 billion for aid while the volume of debt owned to these donor states was $2.7 trillion, 25 times of the volume of the aid (World Bank, 2008, "Key Development Data and Statistics"). In contrast, the accumulation of wealth by the well-heeled population sees no end. By the end of the previous century, 20 percent of the richest population in the world was already consuming 86 percent of the global goods (United Nations Development Program, "Human Development Report 1998," 1998).

Disparities of all kinds have affected both the developed and developing societies. Each day, 26,5000 children, mainly in developing countries, die due to poverty (Global Issues, 2008, "Causes of Poverty"). Poverty has a direct effect on every aspect of human lives. On nutrition, for example, according to a 2006 estimate by the Food and Agricultural Organization, about 854 million, or 12.6 percent, of the world's population are undernourished (World Hunger Education Service, 2008, "World Hunger Facts 2008"). In one estimate, about 27 to 28 percent of the children in developing countries are underweight or stunted (See Global Issues, 2008, "Poverty Facts and Stats"). And this problem is not limited to the populations in resource-poor countries. In the United States, the largest economy on earth, in 2006, about 37 million people were in poverty (Global Issues, 2008, "Causes of Poverty"). In another estimate, about 10.9 percent of households are food insecure, which was an 11 percent increase over 2005, and about 33.5 million Americans live in food insecure households (America's Second Harvest, 2008, "Learn about Hunger"). In the same year, about 17.4 percent of children were in poverty in the United States (America's Second Harvest, 2008, "Learn about Hunger").

Disparities also affect access to other fundamental elements of social life, such as water, energy, education, etc. Access to water has also become a serious issue for the global poor (Global Issues, 2008, "Poverty Facts and Stats"). It was estimated that 1.1 billion, or one-sixth, of humanity lacks adequate access to water and 2.6 billion, or 40 percent, lacks basic sanitation. And this problem mainly affects the poorest in that two-thirds of the poor live under $2 a day and one-third lives under $1 a day. The toll of water on health and sanitation is grave. About 1.8 million children die a year due to diarrhea and about 5 percent of the GDP, or $28.4 billion, in Sub-Saharan countries was lost due to sanitation issues (United Nations Human Development Program, 2006, "Human Development Report 2006"; see also Global Issues, 2008, "Poverty Facts and Stats"). Only 20 percent of the poorest population has access to water. On education, about 72 million children of primary school age were not in school in 2005 and 57 percent of them were girls (United Nations, 2007,"Millennium Development Goals Report 2007"). Nearly 1 billion, or 17 percent, of people entering the 21st century cannot sign their names (UNICEFF, 1999, "The State of the World's Children"). About 1 billion, or 16 percent, of humanity lives in slums (United Nations, 2007, "Millennium Development Goals Report 2007"). On energy consumption, about 2.5 billion people, or 40 percent, of humanity (including 80 percent in Sub-Saharan nations, or half of the population in China and India), rely on biomass (fuelwood, charcoal, or animal dung) for cooking (United Nations, 2007, "Millennium Development Goals Report 2007"). In contrast, the increasing use of oil for economic growth by industrialized states and newly emerging markets has accelerated environmental degradation, causing global warming and climate irregularities. While the well-heeled populations lavish their spending to fulfill their energy needs, about 1.6 billion, or 25 percent, of the world's people live without electricity (United Nations, 2007, "Millennium Development Goals Report 2007"). The world's spending on the conflict far exceeds our spending on human capital building. In one estimate, only one percent of global spending on weapons was sufficient to put every child in school in 2000 but did not happen (Internationalist, February 1997, "State of the World."). Each year, there are about 350 to 500 million people affected by malaria, and 1 million will die. Africa is the major victim of malaria, with 90 percent of African adults and 80 percent of African children affected by malaria each year (United Nations Development Programme, 2007, "Human Development Report 2007"). Beyond the publicized diseases of HIV and malaria, the world's poorest in more than a hundred countries in Africa, Asia, and Latin America receive little treatment for their suffering of other neglected diseases, such as ascariasis, hookworm infection, trichuriasis, lymphatic filariasis, onchocerciasis, schistosomiasis, and trachoma, despite the fact that these diseases are largely treatable (See Global Network of Neglected Tropical Diseases, 2006, "About Neglected Tropical Diseases"). Overall, it was estimated that about 1 billion, or 16 percent, of humanity are suffering from the neglected diseases (NTDs) (World Health Organization, 2008, "Control of Neglected Tropical Diseases"). Overall, on the important indicators of human development, such as equitable growth, life expectancy, infant and child mortality, and literacy and education, there was a decline in the 1980-2000 period, when compared to the 1960-1980 period (Wisebrot, Baker, Kraef, and Chen, 2001).

In this imbroglio of global underdevelopment, the major victims are the vulnerable excluded people, such as the poor, the victims of inter-group differences or environmental injustice and victims of wars and conflicts, and etc. In this development model where very few have gained, the vast majority of the people have been excluded from the fruits of the so-called "modern development." The vulnerable populations find themselves not only deprived of all the tangible economic resources but also see the loss of their intangible community capital. This community capital is most crucial to their survival when they are deprived of everything else.

As a result of these fanatical competitions, the world has seen little progress in the well-being of those vulnerable groups. The much touted achievements in science and technology have only benefited some. Or to be more precise, the only beneficiaries of our collective wisdom and ingenuity are the well-off populations in the world. Yet even there, there is a deficit of community capital for the underprivileged.

Most of the poor populations, especially those in the non-industrialized countries, rank at the bottom in any human development indexes, such as in life expectancy, maternal health, infant mortality, nutritional adequacy, and access to life opportunities. For a long span of modern history, even with the uplifting aspirations outlined in the UN Declaration of Human Rights, those underprivileged remain invisible on the development screen of the strong states. Their invisibility naturally results in little progress and improvement in our development dilemma. This dilemma has not escaped the scrutiny by such development critics as Raul Prebisch, Andre Gunder Frank, Immanuel Wallerstein, and Joseph Stiglitz (Frank, 1967; Prebisch, 1950; and Stiglitz, 2003.)

It was obvious that the dominant development practices and their derivatives have not really made sustainable changes in the development of those invisible populations. It is even fair to say that prior to the global health crisis, especially the HIV/AIDS epidemic, there was not substantial progress in international sustainable development.

Summing up the failure of the conventional thinking about development, there are several key problems. First, the concept of development is fraught with contradiction and hidden agendas. The problem starts with the definition of development. Most development theories and practitioners have subscribed to a uniformed definition and measure of development. That is, development is about competition for military and financial prowess against other nation states. Development is equated to "exhaustive" materialism and consumerism, which has been perpetuated at the expense of environmental integrity. There is little discussion on how community capital could be sustained to benefit all. The community capital is made up of solidarity mechanisms or positive social, cultural, and health knowledge or practices that nurture the growth of human capital. Second, the benefits of innovations have not been shared by all and in fact, inequities between the haves and have-nots are enlarging in every aspect of global development. There is an increasing "spiral of silence" or "blindfoldism" in the face of inequities. The growing wealth disparity among nation states and within nation states provides strong evidence that only a small proportion of humanity has benefited from the fruits of life-improving inventions. By 2008, in a context of high inflation and decreasing resources, the concentration of wealth is only going to be even more polarized. In the United States, the middle class are experiencing very large difficulty in staying in that class because their means and belongings are being translated into even larger collaterals to the lending agencies. Third, development is driven by ideological competition or political calculations, instead of practical assessment of needs in the affected communities. In global health, one of the most prominent examples is ex-president George W. Bush's emphasis on "sexual abstinence" in the aid programs for HIV prevention, at the risk of increasing prevalence of the disease. The other example is the debate on universal health care in the United States. In this debate, the need to improve very large health disparities in the United States was eclipsed by the superficially created, negative labeling of "socialized medicine" in the reference to universal health care. For almost a hundred years, this relentless rivalry between the proponents of socialism and capitalism or among different religious factions has brought about many large-scale tragedies, such as the mass casualties under Stalin and Mao Dze-tung as well as the unjustifiable wars in Vietnam, Afghanistan, Iraq, and so on. Consequently, this old development model has failed to bridge differences. Diversities and differences that could have been the source of ingenious solutions have been negatively exploited to their maximum for political gains for dominance. What is worst is that humanity has failed in our ability for self-reflection and creative imagination to resolve these challenges. We have failed to recognize that our worst enemy is not a given nation state or a block of "evil states." We share the same environment that is the major source of our survival and we share a common destiny. If there is a common enemy, it is our collective failure in generating sustainable solutions for all the problems of our own making in the following of the misleading development model.

What global health problems have exposed are not just the growing threats of isolated cases of new diseases or epidemics but the fact that we are facing dire challenges in the sustainable development of humanity. The question that the conventional development paradigm has never answered is: "To where does this path lead us?" In the past, some critics mentioned "underdevelopment" for those groups or nation states that might lose out in the competition as a possible consequence. However, today, that term is a euphemism compared to the reality. If no changes are made in our current development model, the only possible scenario is the reduction of humanity. And, here are several possible processes through which this scenario could occur. First, competition for dominance gives rise to micro-conflicts that eventually lead to an apocalyptic scenario, triggered by a marginalized group using nuclear weapons. This could occur in the form of military/nuclear confrontation, economic meltdown, or terrorist attacks. Second, natural disasters and epidemics or pandemics could bring about dire consequences to population health. Third, the exhaustion of natural resources could create intensified global competition or economic hardships. Of course, the history of humanity has demonstrated that there is no linear path for development and there is no foregone conclusion of on the future of humanity. With ingenuity, determination and collective effort, humanity has always triumphed over challenges time and again.

Given the aforementioned discussions, it is obvious that what we need today in addressing global health challenges is *a re-thinking* about our development path from this point on. That is, global health architecture is about the architecture of global development. Therefore, the goal of this book aims to present an alternative conceptual framework to resolve global health problems by tackling the root causes embedded in the global development dilemma.

To fulfill this goal, Chapter 2 presents an alternative global health and development model that is based on the inclusive sustainable development theory, which includes such discussions as inclusion, community capital, inclusive dialogue, and the Hexagon of Partnership Model. Chapter 3 demonstrates the application of this architecture in the discussion of the security of the fundamental elements of life, such as food and energy. Chapter 4 focuses on one of the most critical elements of global sustainable development, water security. In the end, this book aims to illustrate that revitalizing our imaginative power to connect and collaborate is the ultimate solution to global health and development challenges.

Chapter 2

Inclusive Sustainable Development Theory and Hexagon of Partnership Model

Most of the challenges in sustainable development facing humanity today, such as environmental breakdown and global conflicts, are brought about by the misleading assumptions in the conventional model of development. Given the negative consequences of the "old" way of thinking global development, we need a different framework in re-configuring our path of development. This chapter aims to present a new Inclusive Sustainable Development Theory as the conceptual basis to map out global health and development architecture. This framework includes the discussions of the fundamentals of development and the guiding principles of global partnerships in bringing about solutions.

Relevance of Agricultural Community

To disentangle the complex problems of development today requires an analysis of the development progress. A useful starting point is to examine how *homo sapiens* have survived evolutionary challenges. The insights from the history of humanity as to how our ancestors survived the harsh conditions in the natural environment could reveal crucial information about solutions to our development dilemma. Several observations about the human history are relevant here. According to a widely accepted theory, *homo erectus*, the origins of the ancestors of humanity, *homo sapiens*, left Africa about 60,000 to 80,000 years ago and began to live a life of settled communities for agricultural subsistence about 10,000 years ago (See Wikipedia, "Recent African Origin of Modern Humans, 2008; Wikipedia, "History of Agriculture," 2008; Oppenheimer, October 2003).

It is obvious that agriculture has played a central role in the organization of human societies and creation of human civilization, according to Diamond (1997) Diamond has argued that development of human society requires agriculture. Therefore, it is important to recognize certain advantages of agricultural community organization that have promoted the sustainable progress of humanity. Although it is difficult to imagine the agricultural life style of 10,000 years ago, one could gain a clue from the communal living in the rural and indigenous communities throughout the world. It is obvious that despite the advantages of the industrial society in material well-being and efficiency, agricul-

tural organization upholds certain values and follows certain rules that are con-
ducive to the health of a community. First, community plays a central role in the
lives of individuals. Community networks provide the links for individuals to
obtain critical support. The community works as a team. The mutual help
mechanisms are used in every aspect of social life, from caring for children, the
elderly, and the sick, to the guarding of community security. Second, there is an
attitude of reverence for nature and the use of natural balance in farming. For
example, the crops are rotated to provide the needed nutrients in different crops
or to enrich soil. Third, the norms of communal living center on preservation,
instead of un-renewable consumption, to avoid wastefulness. In this regard, the
communal life of the American Indians is also a relevant case in point. Fourth,
agricultural life aims for self-sufficiency. Certainly, it is not to say that agricultural organization has no disadvantages and is the ultimate utopia for human life.
The point is that we can learn certain lessons from the traditional agricultural
community, not the modern super-size, pesticide-empowered industrial farming,
about how it preserves community and environmental capital.

Defining Sustainable Development

In a sense, the solidarity mechanisms and materialistic attitudes provide
some relevance to the discussion of sustainable development. To begin with, it is
important to examine what constitutes "sustainable development" of humanity.
According to a widely used UN definition, sustainable development is a mode of
development that "meets the needs of the present without compromising the
ability of future generations to meet their own needs."(United Nations, "Report
of the World Commission on Environment and Development," 11 December
1987). First, human needs may include a wide range of things, such as
biological, material, social, communal, spiritual, cultural, emotional, and
environmental needs, and the way in which needs are expressed may vary from
community to community. Second, we need to maintain a balance between our
current needs and the needs of future generations so that a given generation is
not "cashing in on" the livelihood of the future generations. Third, the
fulfillment of needs has also to be measured in the context of the amount of
means at our disposal. Several facts are relevant. The total world population is
the highest in human history, and the rate of development is also the fastest. As
of 24 June, 2008, the world's population has reached 6,705,635,887 and is likely
to reach 9 billion by 2042 (See Worldometers, "Current World Population." 24
June, 2008; see also US Census Bureau, "World Population Information," 24
June, 2008). The rapid growth of world population has put considerable strains
on the world's already dwindling resources. As each day goes by, humanity is
facing a larger and larger crisis in accessing food, clean water, oil, energy, and
land. The food crisis reaches its peak and between 2005 and 2008, food prices
have increased by 83 percent, according to the World Bank (Global Issues.
"Global Food Crisis 2008," 2008). As of March 2008, average world wheat
prices have experienced an increase of 130 percent in one year; soy prices saw
an increase of 87 percent higher, rice prices have increased by 74 percent, and
maize has climbed by 31 percent (Holt-Giménez and Peabody. "From Food

Rebellions to Food Sovereignty: Urgent Call to Fix a Broken Food System,"16 May, 2008). The crisis is believed to be caused mainly by irregular climate patterns, the increasing consumption of food and natural resources from the high-growth developing countries, such as India, China, and Russia, increasing use of food for fuel production in developed country (especially in the United States), and a drastic increase in oil prices (See related comments in Financial Times. "Food Crisis is a Chance to Reform Global Agriculture," 30 April, 2008; see also Wikipedia, "2007–2008 world food price crisis"). The food shortage has caused increasing instability in developing countries, such as Mexico, Italy, Morocco, Mauritania, Senegal, Indonesia, Burkina Faso, Cameroon, Yemen, Egypt, and Haiti (Holt-Giménez, and Peabody, "From Food Rebellions to Food Sovereignty: Urgent Call to Fix a Broken Food System," 16 May, 2008). For example, in Haiti, the food prices have increased about 50 to 100 percent within a year and have caused serious social unrest, leading to the ouster of the prime minister (Global Issues, "Global Food Crisis 2008," 2008). The World Bank has predicted that if there is no immediate food aid, about 100 million worldwide will be in the category of the undernourished (World Bank. "Food Price Crisis Imperils 100 Million in Poor Countries, Zoellick Says," 14 April, 2008). The other crisis that has not caught the world's attention but has taken a severe toll on humanity is the decreasing access to clean water. According to *Nature* (2008), more then one billion people in the world do not have access to clean water, and it is estimated that the situation will get worse and the average supply of water per person will decrease by a third in 20 years (Nature, "Global Water Crisis," 2008). In addition to food and water, the imminent crisis facing humanity is the energy insecurity brought about the fear of the decreasing oil reserves. Many fear that once oil reaches its peak production, which can occur as soon as 2010, a drastic increase in prices would be inevitable (Russell and Davis, 10 November, 2007). The oil crisis has aroused the most concern because oil has been instrumental in the economic growth of the industrialized countries and fast-growing developing countries. The other fact that worsens this picture is a lack of other energy choices that could immediately replace oil in sustaining industrial growth. These crises have clearly illustrated that our current path is not sustainable because all these critical and fundamental elements are in the process of being "exhausted," and the fight for controlling these resources has further contributed to increasing global conflict, further weakening the prospect of sustainable development.

The Triangle of Development

To plan the kind of global action needed for sustainable development, it is important to know the drivers of development. The major drivers are actions to improve the negatives in social environment, natural environment, and policy and political leadership. In this writing, these three drivers are termed as a development triangle. Most of the global health and development problems can be attributed to deficiencies in these areas. In social environment, the most important determinant is social inclusion. Social exclusion derives from the discussions of poverty and social determinants of health. According to Wang and Nantulya (2008), among all the social determinants, social inclusion plays the most important role in global sustainable development because most of the development problems today have been brought about by the exclusion of groups or communities from accessing resources, rights, or gains in innovations; or of exclusion of the consideration for other species and other living mechanisms in our management of the ecosystem. According to Wang's (27 January, 2005) original discussions, social exclusion is defined as "the factors and forces at macro- and micro-levels of social life that lead to the weakening or disappearance of critical/positive links to certain populations in accessing rights, resources, and opportunities and that cause a process of marginalization or alienation of the communities to which these populations belong" (Wang, 27 January, 2005, p. 1). The dimensions of social exclusion include wealth gap and chronic poverty, gender inequity, inter-group differences and environmental injustice (race/ethnicity, cast, class, religion, stigma status, rural-urban divide, etc.), and gap in community capital (See Wang and Nantulya, 2008).

Besides social environment, the way in which we manage the natural environment also plays a crucial role in the survival and growth of humanity. As mentioned in the previous chapter, the recent climate irregularity has caused the increase of environmental refugees in the world, and the prevailing scientific opinion is that the major causes for this climate irregularity are man-made factors, such as the increase of carbon dioxide that has increased the green- house effect causing global warming (Intergovernmental Panel on Climate Change, "Climate Change 2001: The Scientific Basis," 2001). This climate change is deemed a contributing factor to such natural disasters as floods, hurricanes, or droughts that have brought an even larger impact on our access to food and water. In mid-June, 2008, the flood along the Mississippi River, the worst since 1993, covering more than 3 million acres of land, severely affected America's farm belt in the midwestern states of Illinois, Indiana, and Iowa. This flood was expected to have a significant impact not only on the national economy in the United States but also on the world's food prices because the region is a major center of production in grain, soy, cattle, pigs, eggs, food processing, shipping, and farm machinery manufacture" (See *Los Angeles Times*, "Midwest Floods' Economic Fallout Uncertain," 22 June, 2008; see also Reuters. "U.S. Midwest Farmland Flooding Boosts Food Prices," 17 June, 2008). Mismanagement of the natural environment has a direct impact of global health in that climate irregularity has facilitated the spread of diseases or epidemics.

Today, the most important element necessary to change our development path is policy and political leadership and it has a two-way interaction with social environment. Action resulting from misguided policy and leadership can produce a very negative impact on global development. Examples abound in this area. The collaborative vision between Nelson Mandela and Frederik Willem de Klerk has single-handedly moved South Africa from a polarized state haunted by apartheid to a nation of reconciliation. The leadership of Uganda's president Yoweri Kaguta Museveni in the fight against HIV/AIDS prevents the disease from becoming a national disaster. Uganda is one of the African countries that had the HIV/AIDS transmission under control before it became a national disaster. Conversely, President George W. Bush's stubborn insistence on the initiation of the Iraq War on the basis of seriously false intelligence has brought about eight years' of endless conflicts and instability to the world. His apathy to peace building internationally and indifference to the global warming phenomenon has not only contributed to elevated national debt for the United States but most importantly a loss of national reputation from which it might take years for the country to recover (Washington Post, "He's The Worst Ever," 3 December, 2006). Leadership matters in the development of humanity. These cases have demonstrated that imbalance or deficiency in the triangle of development leads to problems in global health and development.

A New Theory of Global Development

To redress the ills generated by the "old" way of thinking of development, this writing proposes an inclusive equilibrium theory to describe an alternative thinking about development that focuses on long-term preservation of humanity without compromising the integrity of the community and natural environment. To begin with, in this framework, sustainable development is defined as "the progress of humanity that is measured by the balance and harmony in the long-term growth of individuals, community, and natural environment" (Wang, . "Toward a New Theory of Social Exclusion, Community Capital, and Global Health," 27 January, 2005, p. 1). Excessive inequities in social lives, diseases, inter-group conflict, and environmental degradation would further diminish the community capital needed to achieve sustainable development.

Major Postulates of the Theory

In light of this definition, several premises are built into this theory. First, the growth of humanity is measured by multiple dimensions, which includes balanced growth in economic, cultural, social, and, in particular, in environmental spheres of life in both quantitative and qualitative terms. The positivist tendency to measure progress in terms of quantitative economic fashion needs to be revised. Growth in human development should not be measured only by rates or percentages but also by improvement of the quality of human lives. Take education as an example. The success of education is not simply measured by the number of students enrolled in the schools but by whether students can use the skills taught to generate meaningful and secure livelihoods for themselves. The quality of education is the core of the matter in defining development. Along the same line of reasoning, the measure of GDP does not fully reflect economic progress. For example, Costa Rica, which has a much smaller GDP than the United States, has a longer average of life expectancies. According to a study, the difference between the GDP per capita for Costa Rica and the United States is about $21,000 but Costa Rica's life-expectancy, 76.6, exceeds that of the United States, about 76.4 (Daniels, Kennedy, and Kawachi, 2000). Another report shows that shows that the United States ranked 29[th,] behind the rankings of East Asian countries in the measure of infant mortality (Centers of Disease Control and Prevention, "Recent Trends in Infant Mortality in the

United States," October 2008). This evidence shows that numerical "winnership" is not equivalent to success in sustainable development.

This is not to say that economic growth, as measured in financial terms, is not important, but when economic growth creates excessive inequities, it poses a major challenge to sustainable development because eventually societies as a whole have to pay for the financial or social cost of these different forms of inequities. Today, the challenge is for the global leadership to choose the kinds of economic growth that are sustainable over those that are not.

In this sense, the highest level of progress of humanity *is balanced growth that generates even more resources for generations to come*, or, the renewable growth," in contrast to the "exhaustive growth." For a long time, the believers of the winnership model, have practiced "exhaustive growth." The goal has always been to conquer, subjugate or weed out other groups to appropriate the resources until the desired resources are exhausted. Then the winner moves on to the next target and repeats the same pattern of conquering. However, throughout human history, there were examples of the alternatives.

The most relevant case in point is the indigenous people in the Americas. Since the arrival of Columbus in the Americas, the indigenous have faced serious odds of survival because of the intentional or unintentional extermination tactics employed by the new immigrants. During the past four hundred years, the European immigrants massacred the indigenous, occupied the indigenous land, and even forcefully took their children to attempt to acculturate these indigenous offspring to the Western way.These tactics have resulted in the decimation of more than 50 million of indigenous people in the Americas (See Wang and Nantulya, 2008). Yet today, the importance of the indigenous knowledge of ecological management, environmental preservation, and herbal medicines provides crucial information for our future survival, given the crisis of resources shortage that humanity is facing today. Their minimalist life style has been instrumental in preserving the integrity of the world's environment and natural resources. Throughout human history, traditional indigenous farming method is instrumental in soil preservation (Interview with Felipa, Director of Mujeres en Action. 14 January, 2007). Decimating the indigenous or destroying their cultural heritage would mean a severe loss to humanity and could limit our knowledge repertoire for generating environmental solutions.

In this respect, the winnership model is ill-suited for global development because the criteria of competition in the conventional development paradigm, as reflected in colonialism or the current globalization game, have failed to account for the diverse capabilities embodied in different communities or groups, while, in fact, diversity is the rule of the natural world as well as in human society. Without diversity and the natural balancing mechanisms embodied in diverse organisms, the natural world could not be able to generate and regenerate. The food chain is a perfect example. Without the balance and counterbalance tendencies and mechanisms in the natural world, there are likely constant threats to the survival of micro-organisms, plants, and animals.

In a way, the functioning of human society resembles that of the natural world. The diverse human knowledge, capacities, and experiences add to our ability to resolve problems and innovate. The fear and discomfort with diversity as expressed by some fundamentalist political groups, echoes the assumption of the conventional paradigm that global development is a competitive sport and only one single actor dominates in the development process. However, when one single actor dominates at the expense of other parties, the abuse and misuse of power would become an even more grave danger, as the Iraq War has demonstrated.

Second, this new theory sees global community as an *mutually reliant and interdependent* entity and that *peace* is the cornerstone of sustainable development. The measure of real progress in development is whether we can transcend the conventional methods of dealing with conflict to produce sustainable peace. Instead of indulging in an endless cycle of revenge and mutual annihilation, reconciliation that leads to lasting peace is an indispensable element of sustainable development. This thinking is not political naiveté, as the old guard supporting the Cold War might declare. It is feasible and it is the real measure of progress in development. The case of South Africa in ridding itself of its apartheid system is a relevant case in point. To this end, one of the most critical links in peace building *is inclusive dialogue*. Sustainable peace building requires us to minimize the negative impact of ideological difference through constructive communication that includes all stakeholders. As tempting as it is, we need to cease the practice of the "creation of a virtual enemy" or the "blaming game" in all levels of global relations. The great peacemakers, such as Martin Luther King or Gandhi, have demonstrated that we cannot not communicate to resolve our differences and peace building is not a naïve undertaking. What we have learned in the human history is that dialogue for peace, backed by a strong collective will, should always be our first resort and the best preventive strategy in resolving global conflict. Despite the expediency and immediate satisfaction of a quick use of force, the chain reaction from the use of a conflict-prone strategy is often beyond the control of the perpetuator. And a thoughtful government should never forget that the victims of the invincible governments' rivalry are the ordinary vulnerable people.

After the Second World War, the exercise of defining evil and good has been a difficult exercise because it is intertwined with other complexities. For example, the confrontation between different sides of the Cold War might be perplexing to the post-modernist thinkers. During the Cold War, Hu Chiming of Northern Vietnam was seen as the arch enemy of the Western countries while most failed to recognize that Hu was seen a great liberator by his countrymen. Hu was seen as an anti-colonialism leader who single-handedly moved the country from the yoke of imperialism to independence. Despite the very controversial methods that Hu undertook to address social equity, North Vietnam under Hu brought about universal education, economic equality, and universal health care to its people. These ideals were not too different from those valued by the Western socialist democracies.

The same thing can be said about Cuba. The ideological war fought by the West against Cuba was bewildering because in many measures of social and population health, Cuba fares much better than most developing countries in health care, gender equity, and social equilibrium. Yet Cuba also replicates the same pitfalls of many democratic or non-democratic countries in the area of the concentration of political power and the limitation of freedom of speech. Despite the negative image of Castro in the Western media and the mode of dictatorship exercised, Castro has also been seen by most of his own people as a success that has moved the country from chaotic colonial rule to a state that values population health and universal education.

The scenario is similar in China. Despite the attempt of many to demonize China, one cannot deny the Chinese modern historical experience has consolidated its "victim" status because of the imperialist invasions against China in the aftermath of the Opium War. The Communist Party, led by Mao Tze-tung, has single-handedly lifted the country out of the curse of poverty and ill health. Just in a matter of 30 years, under Mao's rule, the life-expectancy had doubled in China. Of course, when compared to the industrialized states, China is not perfect in many measures of social progress but this imperfection is not totally of its own making. China, one fifth of the humanity, was under the imperial rule for four thousands of years before they were further threatened by the colonial invaders in the late nineteenth and early twentieth centuries. The Communist revolution was an inevitable choice for China to avoid a total collapse, but China also paid a colossal price for this choice by being isolated by the West. Today, when China has finally decided to move to the ideological center in its social reform by practicing a capitalist-socialism resembling that of other countries, it is perplexing that now China is facing an even harsher ideological bashing from the Western media than before. It is important to remember that China is a victim of an outdated international development model that drives certain polluting industries unwelcome in the West to move their production bases to China. In a sense, China, like many countries in Latin America and Africa, is a victim of environmental imperialism.

Certainly, these countries are far from perfect by the Western standard. Yet in an interconnected and crowded world, the exercise of creating a virtual enemy out of each other does real harm to international relations. The danger of the unilateral, belligerent global strategy lies in the fact that most of these new powers hold critical stakes in global peace, and environmental, financial, and renewable resources solutions.

A related point is that after all, the ideological confrontational strategies have never really worked after the failed confrontations against Communist Vietnam, Cuba, and Soviet Union. The world leaders have to cease recycling a conflict-provoking tactic in resolving hegemonic issues. They have to stop creating semantic deception, such as in the use of "preventive war", in perpetuating their conflict-promoting agenda. And in addition, the flag of conflict is often waged in the name of protecting a state's security and this is the most dangerous excuse used in international relations because, today, the largest security threats facing the world do not come from any individual state but from the forces external to the community, such as environmental disasters, epidemics, and dwindling natural resources.

In the larger picture, humanity shares a common security interest and a common purpose in defending our interests against these external forces. The aggression waged by a few states in the name of self-interest does not reflect the self-interest of humanity.

Third, a related point is that this theory sees development as progress in the ability of humanity to *share resources and the fruits of our innovation*. The deficiency in this area of global development has been the source of the unrelenting competition and inter-group antagonism. In this sense, the real challenge facing humanity is how we move beyond the mode of "plunderism," getting the most for one's fellow kinsmen or ideologues that gives the "winners" the rights to continue, intentionally or unintentionally, exploiting the vulnerable in the development process. A major problem with the "winnership" model of development is that in the process of amassing wealth in an exponential manner, the "winners" have failed to invest in the communities that have paid for the winners' wealth in the first. In a sense, the idea of sharing has been misunderstood and becomes the focal point of a fierce ideological debate between capitalist and socialist disciples. For example, in capitalist countries, (as a matter of fact, there are really no such countries any more in the purest sense of the word), the mentioning of sharing of wealth immediately encounters an ideological firewall because it conjures up the dreadful image of the communist control under Mao or Lenin. As a matter of the fact, if we can borrow from capitalist lingo, spreading wealth can mean "investing in your customers." The continuing polarization of wealth distribution in the world says more about the failure of "renewable" capitalism than the inevitability of socialism. This gap simply means that the means of production have not been invested back in the customers that have helped the viability of the capitalists. And this is the most worrisome phenomenon facing the future of capitalism, not the revival of the Lenin-style socialism.

In the context of rapid decrease of natural resources and exponential growth of population in the globe, the wealth gap has reached a crisis level. Resource disparities are occurring at two levels: within a nation state and among the nation states. For example, United States has seen the highest level of wealth disparities among industrialized states, with a GINI coefficient of 0.47 (with 0 indicating perfect equality and 1 representing perfect inequality.) (See Pathfinder, "Social Stratification in the United States," 2008). China has a similar problem with wealth disparity. In the United States, the percentage of the poor has increased by 14 percent between 1995 and 2004 while 80 percent of the wealth is controlled by less than 10 percent of the population (Wang and Nantulya, 2008; See also Hurst, 2007, 31). In the United States, the wealth gap among racial groups is especially pronounced. For example, an estimate in 2007 showed that the income gap between Caucasian and African American families has widened, and an African American family makes about more than 50 percent of the income of a Caucasian family (National Public Radio. "Income Disparity Persists Between Blacks, Whites." 14 November, 2007). The root causes of wealth gap in the United States have been attributed to several exclusionary factors, such as in education and racial discrimination, which generate an intergenerational effect among the excluded groups (See Wang and Nantuyla, 2008). In China, the wealth gap is related to a rural-urban divide. In other developing countries, the wealth gap can also be attributed to a combination of exclusionary factors. In addition to inter-group discrimination and rural-urban divide, other factors include class and caste, gender, and environmental injustice. Among nation states, the wealth gap is prominent between the resource rich and re-source-poor countries. A UN study on the world's economic activities showed the "developed" countries controlled 90 percent of the world's total direct in-vestment, and the mutual trade and the multinational companies alone owned over 80 percent of the world's total (See the UN study mentioned in People's Daily, "Economic Globalization Widens Wealth Gap: UN Official," 9 June, 2001). In the same study, it also reported that the developed countries, which account for 20 percent of the world's population, had yielded all the technologi-cal innovations while, at the same time, one third of the world's population did not have access to creations at home nor had acquire advanced technologies from abroad (Ibid.). The report also showed shows that the income gap between the world's richest 20 percent of the population and the poorest 20 percent has widened from 30:1 in 1960 to 74:1 in 1997 (UN study mentioned in People's Daily, "Economic Globalization Widens Wealth Gap: UN Official," 9 June, 2001)).

There are several possible consequences of the wealth disparities. In the short term, they could trigger temporary instabilities, such as the food riots that have occurred in more than 33 countries in the wake of the rapid increase in food prices in 2008. In the long term, it could bring about massive discontent that leads to serious social conflicts, revolutions, or wars. In this scenario, the health status and overall well-being of the underprivileged is further threatened when large-scale disasters are accompanied by epidemics. The underprivileged are already suffering a higher level of morbidity and mortality. Therefore, the inclusive sustainable development theory sees resource disparity is a major fac-tor contributing to a lack of global development.

Fourth, this theory sees a "renewable and balanced economy" as a criti-cal element of sustainable development. The main reason is that balanced and renewable growth fosters community capital that prevents instability and con-flict. It means that the political leader does not only cater to the interests of one faction but needs to include the considerations of every group in economic deci-sion-making. For example, some governments of developing countries have been practicing the "exhaustive model" of economic growth that places pollut-ing industries over environmentally friendly economies. In this mode of devel-opment, environmental decisions that favor polluting industries often hurt the interests of the farmers or the environmentalists. Consequently, environmental mismanagement often leads to pollution or shortage, floods, and drought, which ultimately hurts agriculture, on which most of the population relies for liveli-hood. The other case is the development of the auto industry in the United States. For a long time, the US government was under pressure to support the unsustainable growth of an auto industry whose future solely depends on the supply of oil, which is volatile and rapidly dwindling. As the American counter-parts in Europe, Japan, and even China are shifting the development of its auto industry to a model of producing cars that are fuel-efficient and that uses renew-able energy, the US auto industry has gradually lost out in the global market. The protection by the government, especially under Reagan, and both Bush presidents, of one sector's self-interest has actually caused a severe damage to the long-term economic prospects of the country. Given the fact that the auto-related business takes up a relatively significant proportion of American econ-omy, this policy favoring an unbalanced, unrenewable economic model has caused some damage to the long-term development of American economy. The case of the auto industry in the United States has exposed the problem of "subsi-dized capitalism." When an economic decision is made in such a way that sup-ports certain sectors' short-term profit-making against the long-term interest of the majority, "subsidized capitalism" to support unrenewable economy is against the true spirit of capitalism and democracy because it does not value fair play and lets the unsustainable interests of certain people prevail over the sustainable needs of the majority. When the demand for the unrenewable economy is not there, subsidized capitalism can bring about serious economic damage because the rest of populace is now held as its hostage. If the unsustainable economy does not receive further subsidies, its collapse will sink a large number of its affiliates whose subsistence relies on this subsidy scheme as well as creating a rippling effect throughout the whole capitalist system. In this globalized era, it means that this rippling effect is likely to affect everyone.

Fifth, on a related point, this theory sees the use of *a planting strategy over a plucking strategy as the determinant of development.* Literally speaking, a planting strategy generates a multiplication effect. It is like nurturing the soil to help the plant grow well so that the plant bears abundant fruit while, in con-trast, the plucking strategy takes away all the fruit on the trees without putting enriching elements back to the soil (See Wang, *Global Health Partnerships: Pharmaceutical Industry and BRICAs,* 2008).

This metaphor can be applied to most of the situations in global devel-opment. For example, in population health, the fruit is social and population health (in a very broad sense of the word); the nutrients are actions that support the increase of community capital, such as in access to education, poverty reduc-tion and equitable growth, gender equity, and improvement in health care, and the soil is tangible and intangible capital. When the community receives support for balanced growth, their capacities would be enhanced to generate a self-sustained growth. When a health care system makes major efforts to carry out preventive care, such as nutrition, maternal child care, immunizations, regular check-ups, and disease preventions at educational settings and in the workplace, the benefits to the society are often multiplied in terms of the fewer risks in the transmission of diseases, lower rate of morbidity and mortality, and a higher rate of social cohesion and solidarity, which increases the community capital of a given society.

Take pharmaceutical access as another example. A plucking strategy sets a profit threshold and aims to maximize the profits of a given drug by setting the highest price possible, and therefore it has to cater to the needs of those who can afford the drug. A plucking strategy would rather focus on the diseases of the populations in the developed countries or the resource-rich in developing markets because of the assumption that drugs for rare diseases would not meet the investment-return ratio competition. In contrast, a planting strategy sees the diseases prevalent in the resource-poor countries as a grant opportunity for new drug development despite the fact that they might generate less profit margin. A company uses a planting strategy does not mind a much small profit margin for the treatment for the neglected diseases in resource-poor countries because the large volume, or the large number of people suffering from those diseases, is likely to make up for the difference in the calculation of total profit. Or the company might use the research gains from the drug development process to develop other block-busters.

In addition to pharmaceutical access, the planting strategy can also be applied to other areas of development. For example, in economic development, the soil is community while the fruit is business profits. If the government and businesses continue plucking away the wealth from the community without growing the capacity of the community, the growth would not be sustainable in the long run. The critical capacity building includes affordable education, health care, and affordable housing, minimum wage, life-long skill re-tooling, and most importantly a sustainable regulatory framework, such as a fair taxing scheme or fair banking rules. In the hindsight, one of the factors that contributed to the aggravation of the 2008 financial crisis was that there was no effort made to save the 4 million homeowners who were trapped in the sub-prime crisis. The Bush government, supporting financial deregulation, has allowed the banking industry to pluck away the wealth from the community by applying various complex and risky financial schemes on the consumers. The mortgage that those consumers were supposed to pay is a key driver of the profit for the banks and economic growth. In a sense, the mortgage payers have subsidized the large banks' profit. Consequently, when the soil, or the community, is deprived of fertilizers, the fruits or the banks' profit and economic growth, cannot not be sustained.

The other example is the story of successful economic development of the four Eastern Asian "dragons," i.e., Hong Kong, Taiwan, South Korea, and Singapore, that has verified the benefit of this planting strategy. In all four cases, development programs have been designed to increase access to educational opportunities, a major cultural value that is a critical component of the community capital. In this case, education has created a multiplying effect to improve different types of social inequities. It has improved socioeconomic equity; gender equity; and democratic capital. In addition, the four states also have a well-functioned health system that provides quality care to its populace. Taiwan, in particular, has provided high-quality and very affordable universal health care to more than 98 percent of its residents that makes Taiwan stand out even among the industrialized countries.

Sixth, this theory sees sustainable development determined by a gradual, "bottom-up" process of change in community development. Exogenous changes, especially those based on a certain sense of cultural superiority, are doomed to fail. In the face of development hurdles, the communities are those closest to the problems and are most keen in terms of their needs and wants. There are several problems with the interventions led by the outsiders. First, the outsiders might have "impure" motivations. The outsiders' activities in Africa and the Americas have shown that most outsiders tend to impose their biased ideology, be it racial or cultural, on the development agenda of the locals. In colonial days, the self-interest was to obtain the most economic benefits, which directly and indirectly contributed to the suppression of locals' potential. To be more specific, the colonists had aimed to extract the largest labor and productivity input from the locals without regard to their long-term development. Few colonialists have invested in the education and health care of the indigenous in Africa, the Americas or Asia. In addition, a related issue is that even when the outsiders have the objectivity to make the appropriate assessment and diagnosis of the problems, their proposed solutions are not necessarily culturally appropriate or effective. Historical cases abound in the disasters of international development. For example, the case of the social change of Iranian revolution in 1979 has demonstrated that the hastily imposed changes by the outsiders that ignored the domestic social, cultural, and religious dynamic could wipe out the gains of the "modernization" programs.

Under the rule of the Shah, the king of Iran, there was a large wealth disparity between the rich and the poor before 1979, and most of the wealth was owned by one thousand families, including the king and the clergy. The Shah had a different view from the clerics about the role of tradition in Iranian society. The clerics advocated a rigid practice of Islam, which banned tobacco, alcohol, movies, gambling, foreign dress, and supporting a strict dress code of wearing the veil for women, and corporal punishment, such as cutting off a hand. In moving forward with his modernization program, the Shah formed a close tie with the West, especially with the United States, mainly for the sake of sharing the oil profits. The Western presence alerted the religious traditionalists. The presence of the United States reminded Iranians of the imperial intentions of the former British empire while the Shah's support in Iran was fragile, mainly from Iran's upper and middle classes.

Shah's ridicule of the religious traditionalism provoked a strong reaction from the clerics. Shah's remarks that the Iranian society under him was moving into the jet age while the mullahs wanted to remain "in the age of the donkeys" demonstrated a serious cultural divide between the reform-minded government and the religious conservatives. One of the Shah's strongest critics was Ayatollah Ruhollah Khomeini. The Shah's modernization program, which started in 1954, was fiercely opposed by landlords and some clerics, and led to the issuing of the fatwa (religious edict) by Ayatollah Khomeini against the reforms. Facing the crackdown on dissent by the Shah, Khomeini had to go into exile in southern Iraq. The king's increasing violence against the clerics had only driven Iranians closer to Khomeini.

Despite some symbolic benefits, the Shah's reform program had failed to deliver the promise for most Iranians. With the help from the West, mainly the United States, the Shah's reform program had brought about some initial benefits to both Iran and United States. Iran's less antagonistic position toward Israel had helped reduce some tensions in the Middle East while the United States had gained from a more stable supply of oil. The United States was instrumental in expanding Iran's nuclear capacity as well as its economic growth. The major indicator of the growth was the expanded production of oil. Yet these economic reforms had not spread to all Iranians evenly. Corruption and inflation had actually cancelled out the gains for the majority of the Iranians. The large gap remained between the haves and have-nots. At the same time, Shah intensified his repression of the clerics who opposed his modernization. Besides economic reform, other social and cultural reform measures added fuel to an already intense conflict between the Shah and clerics. These other measures include censorship of the books of Islam in 1966 and reducing the power of the religious sector in deciding family matters, especially involving women's rights. The Shah also mandated laws to give women more say in marital affairs. The most provocative reform was that in 1976, when the Shah ordered replacing the old Islamic calendar with a new secular calendar. In contrast, Khomeini's vision for Iran was in line with the Muslim fundamentalism, where spiritual teachings would offer guidance for the political, economic, and cultural aspects of Iranian society.

The Shah's contempt for and brutal repression of religious traditionalism eventually led to the ouster of his regime. The Shah and his family went into exile on 16 January, 1979. After 11 February, 1979, Khomeini returned to power and established a government ruled by Islamic Sharia, which ordered the removal of non-Islamic elements from the public and private sectors. In addition, he also banned the Western influence, such as gambling or drinking, in the cultural and social milieus of the Iranian society. Strict observance of the fundamentalist teachings of Islam was imposed. For example, women were segregated from men; women were ordered to retreat from public life; women had to wear a veil. Mandatory school prayers were instituted. Khomeini also cut Iran's ties with the West (Macrohistory and World Report, 2007; see also Wikipedia, 2008, "Iranian Revolution"). In a matter of days, the Western-looking Iranian society became a secluded community and became one of the most antagonistic rivals to the West.

In this case, the failure of the reform was not difficult to comprehend. The major cause of the failure is that it was a top-down process of change; it was not culturally appropriate; it never received support for the critical opinion leaders or to be more precise, the key stakeholders were excluded in the political process. And most important of all, the reform was borrowed and transplanted from an exogenous model of change and its premises were full of negative implications of cultural imperialism.

The other example is the encouragement of the use of formula to replace breast milk for the mothers in developing countries (See RALPH [The Review of Arts, Literature, Philosophy and the Humanities], "Breast vs. Bottle,

Part I," 2003-2004). In the 1960s, several factors converged and led to the use of bottle milk to replace breast milk for infants in developing countries. These factors include the increase of working women in the cities; the influence of Western cultural values on the educated in the developing countries; and the promotion of bottle milk by Western companies. Many educated or working women were persuaded by advertising while it associated formula with infant health and linked that to a status symbol, as indicators of prosperity and modernity. In the hospitals, sales representatives, under the title of milk nurses, received commissions for promoting manufacturers' products to new mothers in the hospitals. The promotion of bottle milk was also facilitated by development agencies. For example, the United Nations Children's Fund (UNICEF), among the major development agencies, helped legitimize substitute food in developing countries in the 1960s. However, there was some suspicion in the public health community that bottle milk was correlated with stagnant growth, malnutrition, or even death among infants. In fact, two leading pediatric public health specialists, Derrick Jelliffe and Patrice Jelliffe, regarded the use of powdered milk by feeding programs in the 1940s and 1950s as a "nutritional tragedy." It was noted that bottle-fed infants suffered more nutritional imbalance than breast-fed ones and were more vulnerable to bacterial and viral infections and parasites in their second year. Marasmus, a severe growth failure syndrome, was suspected to be associated with the use of bottle milk. In the face of a lack of access to sanitized bottles and water, formula-feeding also contributes to infections, especially diarrhea, and diseases that could lead to lead to malnutrition and other health problems. It was also noted that bottle milk does not offer the same protective elements as breast milk. The contrast between the 12 percent of infant mortality among breast-fed infants and the 95 percent among bottle-fed infants in seven villages in the Punjab studied in the 1950s showed a very high risk of bottle milk to the health of newborns See RALPH. "Breast vs. Bottle, Part I." 2003-2004).

In the face of Derrick Jelliffe's criticism of "commerciogenic malnutrition" in Jamaica and damaging statistics in the 1970s, social activists were able to exert pressure on the major producer of bottle milk, Nestlé, and the passing of the World Health Assembly to adopt the UNICEF's International Code in May 1981 that restricts the advertising and the distribution of milk samples in health care facilities. But it is believed that the code has not been strictly enforced. In many developing countries, hospitals, health workers and mothers still receive free supplies and samples from some companies, and the adornments in the ambiance of the maternity wards, such as posters, calendars, wall clocks, growth charts and other paraphernalia, make suggestive or blatant advertising for particular brands or companies (Baby Milk Action, 22 June, 1998). As a result, the activists renewed their boycotts in 1998. This example shows that the development agenda catering to the interests of the outsiders, often the commercial interest, could have damaging effects on the sustainable development of the vulnerable populations.

Solution at the Macro and Micro Levels

At the operational level, the solution for sustainable development is *inclusion (in an inclusive sense of the word),* as embodied in inclusive partnerships. The premise of inclusion is to recognize the legitimacy and validity of all communities in contributing to and sharing the growth of humanity and in contributing to the solutions of problems. Inclusive solutions in global development include the recognition of diverse cultural backgrounds, ideologies, capabilities, beliefs, values, thoughts, and practices in bringing about effective solutions to development problems.

Inclusive solutions have to do with bridging the gaps in accessing resources, production, consumption, participation and expression in global life. Inclusive solutions are also about reconciling ideological differences among rivaling political, economic, religions, and social groups through a globally monitored and mediated fashion. For example, in global health, specific efforts need to be made in improving the conditions of the vulnerable groups because they are the majority of the global population. And the progress in the population health of the vulnerable tends to have the most profound impact on the long-term development of humanity. The vulnerable groups include, but are not limited to, the chronically poor, underprivileged class/caste, excluded women and men, ethnic/racial minorities, indigenous rural villagers, victims of conflict, and those who are stigmatized or marginalized. For a long time, they have been excluded from accessing resources, rights, and opportunities,

Given the need to achieve inclusion, there are several critical elements in this model of partnership. The major element is *inclusive dialogue.* The importance of communication in various forms to global development has been acknowledged by leading social scientists because communication plays a central role in brining about social change. For example, Dr. Howard Perlmutter, of the University of Pennsylvania, has generated a model of "deep dialogue" in the building of a global civilization (See Perlmutter, "Deep Dialogue." 2006). Perlmutter (2006) believes that deep dialogue competencies are essential in political, social-cultural, scientific, technological, medical and ecological leaders.

In the inclusive partnership model, the starting point is *inclusive dialogue.* There are several assumptions and operating principles in an inclusive dialogue. I. Inclusive communication regards all stakeholders as part of the solution. Therefore, all the stakeholders that can be instrumental in strengthening the positive critical links to a given resolution to a problem should be included in the dialogue process. II. An inclusive dialogue assumes that communication is a multi-channel and multi-dimensional process with the ultimate goal of generating a mutually beneficial solution. III. An inclusive dialogue sees diversities and differences as strengths and assets, not liabilities, to an ultimate solution. IV. An inclusive dialogue aims for groups of differences to find the largest common denominator in the communication process. V. An inclusive dialogue sees empathy as the major communication skill that facilitates the process of inclusive dialogue. The empathy theory stipulates that empathy is a social emotion that individuals experience as a response to the emotions of others (See Dolf Zillmann's empathy theory in *International Encyclopedia of Communication,*

2008). In a word, empathy is the ability for individuals to put themselves in others' shoes. VI. An inclusive dialogue follows a constructive framework of communication that includes the bridging of such factors as: perceived benefit, agency (authority and power) efficacy (resources and capacity); the amount of motivation; convergence of self-interest and stakes; proximity of beliefs, values, cultural and world views (including gender and religious backgrounds) and ideologies; interpersonal rapport; amount of trust; psychological distance in socioeconomic, professional, community and technological experiences among the stakeholders; and degree of convergence in goals. The extent to which these factors are addressed could determine the extent of success in an inclusive dialogue. For example, in addressing global financial crisis, the United States convened a G-20 meeting in Washington, DC, in the middle of November, and this was one of the first few meetings including BRIC countries in a global financial summit. This step of inclusion was important because these four countries account for 41.8 percent of the global population, and they are the fastest growing economies in the world (Eghbal, 5 November, 2008). In contrast to the fact that most Western countries being the "consumer" countries, the BRICs are "producer" countries that have accumulated a large amount of foreign reserves. Without the participation of the BRICs, it is hard to imagine how the developed world can ride out the financial crisis and resolve such challenging issues as "currencies" and "exchange rates," which have all broken down since the Brentton Woods System (Thorpe, 13 November, 2008).

In global health, an example of the challenges in inclusion is about pharmaceutical access for reducing HIV-risks of the poor villagers in resource-poor countries. Important stakeholders/participants for an inclusive partnership in the community are health clinics, government (police, mainstream health system, various government bureaus, etc.), civil society (the rights advocates, NGOs, inter-governmental agencies, charities, etc.), and the private sector (pharmaceutical providers, multinationals, etc.). If a certain critical link to the solution is missing from the communication process in partnership formation, the solution will be imperfect. In one case, a pharmaceutical company asked a UN agency to approach a sex worker group in South Asia to be volunteers for a free clinical trial. In this experiment, the sex workers were asked to take an experimental drug without using any protection when they had intercourse with their clients. The clinical trial aimed to test the preventive effect of the drug against HIV/AIDS. In the face of the risks of contracting HIV/AIDS for the sex workers, the sex workers requested the company to provide some form of health insurance if the sex workers contracted HIV during clinical trial. This request was refused, and the potential partnership was aborted. The failure was obvious because the critical link of human rights advocacy was not included in the formation of the partnership. Therefore, inclusive dialogue is multi-faceted and is designed for community strengthening. It is not a limited dialogue among the elite or "selected leaders" but a multi-direction dialogue that includes all parties that have a stake in a given problem.

The target of inclusive solutions is *community*. In physical and metaphysical sense, community is a common area in which members share identities, characteristics, beliefs, values, resources, risks, preferences, or needs (Wikipedia, "Community," 2008). Global development work should target the balanced growth of a community because for most of the vulnerable people, community provides the tangible and intangible support for their livelihood. In countries where government support does not trickle down to the local levels, community solidarity is the source of survival for resource-poor people.

To preserve the integrity of community requires the maintenance of *community capital*. In general, this is tangible and intangible capital reflected in the development process. The tangible capital is concrete financial investment in a given community, while in contrast, intangible capital is the amount of invisible strength or positive social, cultural, moral or psychological assets embodied in the community that promote peace, equity, and cohesion. Examples of intangible capital can be healthy practices, community solidarity or mutual help mechanisms. In global development, intangible capital plays a large role in areas where investment in financial capital is lacking. For example, the support of the underprivileged and stigmatized is largely voluntary in resource-poor countries. Most of the time, the support derives from community-based mutual-help mechanisms. In Africa, the care of HIV-affected orphans often falls on the shoulders of the relatives, communities, or charities. Without this mutual help mechanism, it is quite impossible for the resource-lacking governments to shoulder the responsibility of caring for all the HIV/AIDS infected and affected orphans.

The community capital is often diminished by social and wealth inequities because disparities create community disequilibrium that can contribute to the increase of crime, resentment, or apathy. Community capital increases "life-sustaining, capacity-enhancing, and resource-multiplying community activities" that can be translated into real community growth (see Wang, 27 January 2005). The major constructs in community capital theory are beneficial ethnic knowledge (in health, environment and biodiversity, nutrition, interpersonal communication and community relations), cultural capital (positive rules [such as caring for the old], norms, and practices), critical links, trust and faith, interdependence, reciprocity, and mutual benefit (see Wang, 27 January 2005). There are several constructs embedded in the formation and increase of community capital (See Wang, 27 January, 2005). First, benefit sharing and reciprocal action increase community capital. Second, valuing a balance between self-interest and community interest increases community capital. Third, strong mutual help mechanisms increase community capital. Examples abound in the world in terms of how community capital sustains or strengthens resource-poor communities. For example, in Thailand, care of HIV patients is often undertaken by Buddhist temples when the government has limited resources to provide comprehensive care. In China, "the provincial mutual help" program has helped provide immediate relief for negative development events. In this program, rich provinces are paired up with poor provinces for development support. In times of disasters, the rich provinces are required to take immediate action to support the disaster relief for the poor ones. This method has proved very effective during the Sichuan Earthquake in May, 2008. In rural Vietnam, poor farmers often organize work units that take turns helping each other in farming.

To preserve community capital requires the consolidation of *critical positive links* that improve development. According to the multiple-link theory (Wang, January, 2005), a critical/positive link provides life-sustaining and protecting resources for balanced and long-term growth of community members. The weakening of the critical/positive links jeopardizes the livelihood and health of community members. Examples of the critical/positive links can be affirmative policies in rights protection (gender, socioeconomic opportunities, political participation and representation, social discourse and cultural expression, labor conditions, and access to health care) and improved access to social resources and upward mobility. Specifically, in health and development issues, examples of critical/positive links are prevention and intervention mechanisms in global peace and security, health, quality education, environmental protection, equitable economic opportunities, and effective governance. Improvement in fundamental subsistence issues, such as peace building, clean environment, food, water, and energy security, is the most critical link for global community.

Concrete examples abound in improving the critical/positive links for vulnerable populations, such as the micro-financing programs by the Grameen Bank in Bangladesh; global development and health programs by the Gates Foundation; the $100-200 computers offered by the One Laptop Per Child Project; the affordable housing project in New York State and New York City (Bill and Melinda Gates Foundation, "Global Development." 2007; "One Laptop Per Child Foundation., 2007; New York City Housing Authority, "NYCHA and HPD Name Developers to Build Affordable Housing Units on Manhattan's West Side," 2007).

On a related point, "connective" thinking is also a crucial cognitive skill in an inclusive dialogue. A connective mode of thinking is the ability to identify the interconnectedness among problems and solutions. For example, global health challenges often are not isolated problems. They tend to have complex interactions with water, food, and energy security, gender equity, poverty, education, environmental breakdown, etc. The solutions that do not take into account this interconnection among the problems are not likely to be sustainable.

Another element in brining about inclusive solutions is the power of *agency*. Supportive agents of development include formal and informal institutions, organizations, and groups. Specifically, they include intergovernmental organizations, government agencies, civil society (such as NGOs, philanthropies, advocacy groups, and so on.), businesses, and transformational leaders.

A Model of Action: the Hexagon of Partnership

Global health and development requires synergizing these architectural elements into a workable solution. To begin with, it is important to differentiate different types of solution for global health and development problems. *A downstream solution* provides immediate relief for the problem at hand, such as diseases, scarcity of basic needs (such as food, water, energy, and temporary shelter), or security threats. For example, in the face of a food security threat, providing immediate food aid is a downstream solution. In the face of an energy crisis, increasing production of oil is only a short-term solution. In the face of an epidemic, providing free medicine is also a downstream solution. *An upstream solution* generates a policy or technical platform to improve the problematic situations. In the example of the food security threat, an upstream solution could be improving the storage conditions or transportation of crops. In global health, an upstream solution could be an improved intellectual property rights framework for accessing life-saving medicines. The DOHA Declaration is a good example.

Beyond downstream and upstream solutions, the most important solution, *a topstream solution* targets the root causes affecting global health and development, such as poverty, inter-group conflict, gender inequity, socioeconomic inequity, community disintegration, and environmental degradation. A good example of the topstream solution is the Millennium Development Goals. For example, in analyzing global energy shortage, it is important to target the fundamental causes. These causes might include geopolitical rivalry, excessive "exhaustive" consumption, irrational "profiteering" and "superficial growth," etc. For example, the reluctance to impose a gas tax on consumers or oil profit tax on the producers has contributed to a carefree consumption pattern worldwide for several decades. The oil crises have done little to change the pattern solely because of the lack of willingness for the political leaders to tell the consumers the truth. The frequently talked about solution of increasing drilling is a dangerously myopic tack that is likely to incur too much harm for the environment to be even considered as a realistic solution.

It is important to note that these different types of solutions are interconnected. Providing downstream solutions without addressing the root causes tends to limit the effectiveness of sustainable development. In essence, the long-term solutions focus on sustainable building in community capita, environmental integrity, and global peace.

Action Guidelines

Inclusive solutions can be carried out by using a Hexagon of Partnership Model. This partnership model maps out six action guidelines to carry out the goals of global sustainable development.

The first action guideline identifies the background of a given global health and development problem and short-term, mid-term, and the long-term solutions. The inclusive dialogue framework is the first step to building the critical links to solutions to a given problem. The framework consists of: I. *Community mapping*. This requires an effort to identify the community needs and the level of community capital in relation to the resolution of the problem. II. *Inclusive partnership mapping*: This requires the identification of the stakeholders who are the critical links to the solutions for the problem, assessing the commitment level of the stakeholders to "inclusive solutions," which includes such consideration as self-interest, level/types of stakes, motivation level, the degree of convergence toward a given goal, and the level of conviction. III. *Agency mapping*. This requires assessing the stakeholders' power of agency (the degree to which they are likely to effectuate a solution, such as leadership or opinion leadership status, authority, resources and capacity available for the solutions; the degree of complementarity; the affective power [the extent of power in mobilizing the public to bring about a change]; their linking power [the amount of connection at multiple level]; technical competence [such as policy making, management, assessment, etc.] to implement an action to carry out a change. IV. *Partnership communication mapping*: this requires examination of the communication factors among stakeholders in the partnership, which includes such considerations as trust, communication effectiveness, interpersonal distance, [such as socioeconomic background, professional background, ideological background, gender, race, and religion, world views, etc]. Communication effectiveness plays a key role in the partnership process.

On the basis of these considerations, a partnership is formed to address a given problem. In this model, a partnership has a higher likelihood of success if there is closer proximity in their level of commitment, agency, linking, and personal rapport factors. The goal of the inclusive dialogue is to find a common denominator in any of these "inclusive dialogue" factors as the starting point of establishing a critical link. Even for stakeholders who have divergent ideologies, world views or political stances, there is still possibility of partnership if they have shared goals or interest or stakes. For example, recently, the insurance business in the United States has become a key partner in support of environmental causes because of the perceived self-interest. Like those victims of unexpected disasters, which, many believe, are the results of environmental degradation, the insurance business is a major victim of these events. In another example, some of the rights-advocacy groups have also started working with their former "nemesis," the pharmaceutical companies, to improve pharmaceutical access for the vulnerable populations because of their sharing of the same goal of improving population health (beyond the self-interest of positive publicity). The fact that they complement each other's capacity also helps in consummating this kind of partnership.

An inclusive dialogue sees the possibility of communication among all parties and in all situations. It does not let ideological differences stand in the way of finding solutions to a given problem. For example, the willingness of the Greek government to provide immediate relief to the victims of the Turkish earthquake in 1999 unexpectedly paved the way for reducing the centuries-old political, religious, and military confrontation. A downstream solution, such as a relief effort, is now translated into sustainable peace-building, a topstream solution.

The second action guideline is, for a given problem, to identify the inclusive dialogue identifies 1. the urgency of different types of solutions, 2. the scope of solutions, 3. the resources needed for a given solution, 4. the timelines for a given solution, and 5. the targeted goal. At this stage, the aim of the inclusive dialogue is to build a unified platform of vision and plans of action. Yet most important of all, it does not generate an isolated solution for an isolated problem. It sees the importance of linking downstream solutions to upstream and topstream solutions. It uses the inclusive dialogue to maximize the potential of a solution to the solutions in other areas. In the inclusive partnership model of global development, there is close proximity in solutions among the key development challenges, such as global peace and security, sustainable environment and renewable economies, food, energy, and water security, and population health.

The third action guideline is for the inclusive partnership to identify the assets and deficiencies in community capital related to a given problem and to consider the ways in which community capacity can be improved to bring about a sustainable solution. For the deficiencies in community capital, the dialogue identifies ways that an inclusive partnership can create, strengthen, or repair the critical positive links vital to a given problem. The strength of the critical links is an important factor in capacity building. The increase of community capital is crucial for the solution to be effective in the long term because the community itself has more stakes in facing the impact of the problem. Community capital can be increased via several paths: investment by the public sector, private enterprise, civil society, or the solidarity mechanisms in the community. The continuing growth of community capital requires the sustained and balanced investment from all sectors. Yet the ultimate goal is to empower the community so that it becomes the major problem solver through improvement of its capacity. A lot of times, the best source of solutions for a community is other communities that have experienced a similar problem. When the capacity of a given community is insufficient, the community-to-community links can provide the most ingenious and timely solution to the problem. For example, as the UNESCO's Cube Project has demonstrated, learning from indigenous farmers is probably more efficient and cost-effective than asking Texas farmers to undergo complex technical training for organic farming. (UNESCO, "CUBES and Spheres, 2002). The other example is the Sichuan Earthquake in China in May, 2008. The community-to-community link proved to be vital in saving lives and re-building the affected communities. In the face of a shortage of such relief items as tents, water, and medicines, the other communities strong in production of these relief items in China took up the task of providing them. Along the same line of reasoning, to resolve inter-group conflict, community contact is probably more effective than government-sponsored action. As mentioned earlier, the case of Greece and Turkey is a most relevant case in point. In the aftermath of the Ismit Earthquake in Turkey in 1999, community contact resolved the centuries-old animosity between those two countries. A similar case was observed in the conflict between Taiwan and China. If it had not been for citizen-initiated actions, mainly those mainland sojourners in Taiwan, the results of increasing exchange of communications, peace dialogue, and mutual visits would not have arrived.

The fourth action guideline is that an inclusive partnership uses a "cross-fertilization" approach to the mobilization and maximization of resources. After a solution for a given problem is fully mapped out, the inclusive partnership identifies possible resources needed for a given task. The resources are derived from tangible and intangible capital. Efficiency is an important concern in the search for capital. Instead of focusing on obtaining new resources, an inclusive partnership looks for ways in which the resources used for other existing solutions can be synergized into the task at hand. At this phase, the partnership aims to integrate the resources among related solutions. In other words, the partnership looks for the links among critical links for solving development challenges because the solutions for development challenges are often interrelated. For example, the partnerships formed to improve food security can also be used for improving other development problems. The process of improving agricultural yield and diversifying crops for small farmers offers an excellent opportunity for addressing other development challenges, such as infrastructure-building, advancement in information technology, micro-financing, nutritional education, occupational health issues in the field (chemical intoxication, parasitic infection, etc.), water safety, organic farming, etc. An inclusive partnership holds a panoramic view when considering the efficiency of using the same critical links for multiple purposes to achieve sustainable development.

The fifth action guideline is for the inclusive partnership to assess the partnership effort through an evidence-based approach by using both quantitative and qualitative measures. The assessment is conducted for two objectives: assessing the *maintenance* (the process) and *the task* (outcome) of the partnership. Effectiveness of the partnership is determined in terms of effectiveness in the interaction between the partnership and the community and efficiency in the interaction among partners. In general, the major areas for assessment include inputs, process, outcomes, impact, and sustainability.

In assessing the maintenance function, the major principles are collaboration, sharing of the risks and responsibilities, community-centeredness, and ongoing assessment. In terms of inputs, we could examine the amount, quality, and effectiveness of communication. On process, the foci should be participation, interaction, communication, coordination, and management. We should examine the management of the communication process and decision-making process in terms of interactivity and the degree of networking. For example, the partnership should follow certain principles, such as honesty, interactivity, openness, reciprocity, respect, transparency, accountability, autonomy, complementarity, convergence of goals, role division, etc. In terms of outcomes, the partnership assesses if the stakeholders have fully exerted their potential or share of responsibility in contributing to the goal of the task. In terms of impact, we assess if the partnership has brought about positive results to a given stakeholder and if that stakeholder has also made the impact that they have intended to make to the partnership. We can also investigate if the partners gain new capacities, expertise, and networks. We can examine if each partner is willing to submit to ongoing performance evaluation and assessment that would help correct the course of action. In terms of sustainability, we can assess if the stakeholders are willing to continue to or participate in the partnership. Communication is the key to the partnership process. An inclusive dialogue framework provides clear communication protocols internal and external to the partnership, especially with regard to conflict resolution and participation effectiveness (See Wang and Nantulya, 2008).

On assessing *task*, in terms of inputs, we need to assess the effectiveness of the operational framework, rules, goals and objectives, and investments. For example, we can evaluate if the goals of the partnership truly reflect the concerns of the community. On the process of executing the tasks, we need to assess if the community are fully included in the operationalization and if the community priorities are respected. On impact, one can examine health status (morbidity and mortality), economic consequences, productivity, and community capacity at the population level. On sustainability, we can assess long-term capacities, governance and accountability, and integration of the results into local policies and social activities. For example, we can assess if there is a follow-up plan for the solutions to take root in the community. We can also examine if the community capital of the targeted community has increased. For example, in HIV prevention and intervention, we can assess if a given community has become more accepting of the HIV infected or affected and is willing to increase voluntary services to care for those affected, or whether the community is equipped with the knowledge, educational or communication capacities to prevent HIV from spreading, or is connected to other communities or institutions to obtain the latest information on prevention and treatment of HIV. Overall, the major goal of assessing the task is to examine if the partnership has achieved specific development outcomes and if the outcomes can be up-scaled or be multiplied.

The sixth action guideline is that the partnership looks into the possibility of scaling up a given solution or linking the short-term solutions to the long-term solutions. An inclusive partnership always adopts a long-term approach to resolve every development challenge. For example, in tackling global food security challenge, the immediate/downstream solution is food aid. Yet for the long term, it requires the integration of work in the whole supply and demand of the food chain, such as balanced macro and micro- agricultural policies (especially in the balance between cash crops and maintenance of small farms), environmental improvement, irrigation regularity, clean and usable water, efficiency in farming, storage and transportation, access to affordable seeds, fertilizers, tools, labor, processing and storage facilities, means of transportation and agricultural and climate informatics, supporting mutual help mechanisms, empowerment of women's participation in agricultural education, and encouraging self-sufficiency, quality and relevant education. Throwing food aid to the starving populations is just a temporary relief and does not help in the long term.

On the whole, inclusive sustainable development theory requires an alternative thinking on global sustainable development, which places collaboration, inclusive dialogue, and mutual help and benefit above the conventional thinking of winnership. In this framework, an inclusive partnership is designed to carry out sustainable development by capitalizing on such strategies as planting or cross-fertilization. This framework will be applied to generating the solutions to the fundamental elements of global development challenges in Chapter 3 and Chapter 4.

Chapter 3

Tackling Food and Energy Security: Community Capital, Inclusive Partnerships, and Multiple-linking

In the face of growing challenges facing humanity, it is clear that solutions cannot remain in the form of political debates or academic exercises. Nevertheless, before solutions can even be proposed, we need to think clearly what the fundamental elements of subsistence are for humanity. The fundamental elements of survival are those things that affect day-to-day living and have long-term implications for population health and development. These are food, usable water, clean air, and clean and renewable energy. And these elements often serve as the best gauge of sustainable development because these elements often affects the largest group of global population, the subsistence farmers. What affects the substance farmers will eventually affect the fundamentals of living for other populations. As mentioned in the first chapter, the root cause of the development problems is exclusion, and exclusion leads to an imbalance of supply and demand/need in the critical elements of life. Since industrialization, the creation of new economies has done little to address the interest of subsistence farmers, who have gradually been excluded from the benefit of globalized economy supported by the major industries or multinationals. Often times, the subsistence farmers become the first victims of the predatory, speculative pattern of the globalized economy. For example, when the oil prices increased rapidly in a matter of months, the subsistence farmers saw a large increase in their cost of production and in the cost of living cost, leading to large-scale famines. The oil price hikes ended up causing large worldwide breakdown of food security, and food riots spread across several continents. Industrial development or the new economies have also failed to address such concerns as to how they impact the environment.

Now, humanity is facing insecurity in each and every of these critical elements of life. It is urgent that we starting correct the past mistakes in development programs by resolving the food, water, and reusable energy insecurity first. This chapter will apply the inclusive sustainable development architecture to analyze the problems and propose solutions for food and renewable energy.

Global Food Insecurity

The food crisis that has occurred between 2007 and 2008 has revived global attention to a problem that has threatened developing countries for decades. Despite the lack of attention to this problem prior to the food crisis, food security is one of most important development challenges facing the globe because it also interests with other pressing issues facing humanity, such as global conflict, energy and environmental challenges, water security, and global health. As formal president of the United States Bill Clinton pointed out, "Food is not a commodity like others. . . ." (FAO. 'Clinton at UN: food, energy, financial woes linked,' 24 October, 2008). In a primitive sense, unlike other consumer items, food is the critical link to survival. In a globalized world, food-producing activities have added functions of improving local economies in resource-poor countries and widening consumer choices in developed societies.

What has happened in the 2007 food crisis reveals that food insecurity is actually the worst form of terrorism that can threaten humanity on such a large scale. It was noted that in 2007 the world price of wheat rose to over $400 a ton, which was the highest ever recorded and was twice the average of the past 25 years (Economist. "Cheap No More." 6 December, 2007). What started out as an isolated event of food price hikes became a global crisis, worsening hunger and causing social unrest that threatens global political and economic stability (See Washington Post. "Global Food Crisis," 26 April, 2008). In one case, after the incessant violent riots in Haiti, Haitian Prime Minister Jacques-Édouard Alexis was forced to step down (Washington Post, "The New Economics of Hunger," 27 April, 2008). In addition to the one billion people who are already living under $1 dollar a day, the crisis has dragged more than 100 million of the world's poorest people deeper into poverty (Ibid.). UN Secretary General Ban Kee-Moon worried that the scope of the crisis had the potential to become a security threat to global political order (Washington Post. "The New Economics of Hunger." 27 April, 2008).

Causes

The food crisis is caused by a combination of factors and if these are not resolved, they are precursors of other even larger crises of similar nature. To begin with, the major cause is a classic case of demand and supply and supply and need imbalance, triggered by a number of factors. These include irregular climate, poor harvests, competition with biofuels, higher energy prices, surging demand in China and India, a lack of long-term land-and-water-management policy, a lack of effective food policies at the global level (agricultural policy, agricultural R&D, land management, food reserves, demand forecasting, trade, and emergency relief). (Washington Post, "The New Economics of Hunger," 27 April, 2008). The immediate cause of the 2007-2008 financial crisis was unexplainable droughts in grain-producing nations, such as the multiyear drought in Australia, which some have attributed to the chronic problem of environmental degradation and global warming. At the same time, the increasing oil prices contribute to the heightened costs of fertilizers, transportation, and industrial agriculture (Economist, "Cheap No More," 6 December, 2007). The encouragement by the US government to use corn to produce ethanol has led to the disincentive for the US farmers to grow wheat and to increase production of corn instead. In

2008, it was estimated that at least a fifth and perhaps a quarter of the U.S. corn crop will be fed to ethanol plants (ibid). What also aggravates the situation is the increasing demand for meat in the emerging markets, especially India and China, which has led to the increasing need for cereals to feed animals (*The Economic Times*, "Now, EU Says Increased Meat Consumption in India, China Driving Food Prices," 6 May, 2008). What has also worsened the situation is the dwindling reserves of grains. In addition, government subsidies designed to protect the agricultural economy, especially in Europe, the United States and Japan, distort further the global food prices. It was noted that the *European Union* provides about $41 billion a year in agriculture subsidies, with *France* being the major beneficiary of about $8.2 billion. The French farmers see that as an indispensable incentive to keep up agricultural production. On the other side of the coin, the global trade favoring high-value products has also caused a distortion of local production patterns in developing countries (*Washington Post*, "The New Economics of Hunger," 27 April, 2008). Adding the fuel to the problem is the speculation on the commodity market (Wikipedia, "2007–2008 World Food Price Crisis").

The recent financial crisis could worsen the situation in several ways. To begin with, given the fact that the epicenter of the crisis is in the wealthy countries, especially the United States and EU countries, their reduced financial power could lead to the decrease of foreign aid the poor countries. Reduced foreign assistance could also force the poor governments to reduce their investment in agriculture, especially for the subsistence farmers. At the same time, the tightening of the credit would exacerbate an already difficult situation for the smaller subsistence farmers (Food and Agriculture Organization. 'Food Outlook," November, 2008). Without bank loans, the farmers could not buy the seeds or fertilizers necessary for their plantings of the new crops. The worsening economic situations, leading to reduced credit, income, and unemployment, might force the poor families to reduce their food budget. This phenomenon was already occurring in 2007, when the number of undernourished increased by 75 million people, increasing to the world total to 923 million (Food and Agriculture Organization. 'Food Outlook," November, 2008).

Solutions

Despite the fact that solutions for food security may vary from country to country, the fundamental solutions at the macro level are similar because the root cause of the challenge is failure in the supply and demand/need balance of food provision in the global community. The major goal for resolving food insecurity, as former President Bill Clinton pointed out, is maximal food self-sufficiency (See Clinton's comments at FAO. 'Clinton at UN: food, energy, financial woes linked.' 24 October, 2008).

First, we also need to identify *the types of solution* necessary for different types of problems. In this case, *downstream solutions* are related to efforts for immediate food relief. *Upstream solutions* are to improve the policy framework at local levels. This would require a well thought-out plan to build the local farming capacity, such issues as financing and credit, agricultural efficiency and effectiveness (technical assistance and capacity building for seed and plant-ing, irrigation and water management, labor and land management, livestock vaccination, etc.), transportation, storage, use of community capital (such as for mutual help mechanisms) and so on. *Topstream solutions* target the root causes of food insecurity at the macro levels, such as conflict, ineffective governance, globalization, chronic poverty, a lack of education, environmental degradation and so on. In specific, the topstream solutions for food insecurity need to take into account existing global agreements in this area, such as the Millennium Declaration, the Johannesburg Declaration on Sustainable Development, the Monterrey Consensus on financing for development, the Rome Declaration on World Food Security (which "reaffirms the right of everyone to have access to safe and nutritious food, consistent with the right to adequate food and the fun-damental right of everyone to be free from hunger"), the World Food Summit Plan of Action (which supports seven commitments to achieve durable food security), World Declaration on Nutrition, Declarations of the World Food Summit: Five Years Later and Other Related Documents, the International Code of Conduct on the Distribution and Use of Pesticides, the Stockholm Convention on Persistent Organic Pollutants, and the Rotterdam Convention on the Prior Informed Consent Procedure for Certain Hazardous Chemicals and Pesticides in International Trade (Food and Agricultural Organization (FAO). "World Food Summit" 2008; see also United Nations. Department of Economic and Social Affairs. January 2008).

Second, once the solution types are identified, we can generate a multi-sector partnerships on the basis of the Hexagon of Partnership Model. The part-nership mapping exercise would generate working partners who have sustain-able interest in the community; who are able to bring about effective operations; who can complement others in the partnership; and who can work together to-ward a shared goal. For the topstream solution of establishing a global policy framework, this partnership should include, but is not limited to, United Nations Food and Agriculture Organization (FAO), major donor countries (such as the United States, European Union, the affected communities, the World Trade Or-ganization, the World Health Organization, UNICEF, the World Bank, regional intergovernmental agencies (African Development Bank, Asian Development Bank, Gulf Cooperation Council, civil society (Grameen Bank, BRAC, Oxfam, CARE, etc.), philanthropies (the Gates Foundation, Ford Foundation, Rockefel-ler Foundation, etc.), multinationals, and so on.

This theoretical framework can be used to analyzing regional cases. Take Kenya as an example. In Kenya, food insecurity is most acutely felt in the eastern and northeastern pastoral districts of Kenya where drought-affected pas-toralists, agro-pastoralists and marginal agricultural farm households depend heavily on the volume of the short rains at the end of the year and in the urban areas where the resource-poor consumers are heavily affected by price fluctua-tion (Kenya Food Security Meeting, "Food Security in Kenya." 2008). It is rec-ognized that most of the downstream interventions, such as food relief, have been effective, but the topstream, development-oriented interventions are inade-

quate (See Kenya Food Security. "KFSSG's Long Rains Assessment Report," 2008"). It is estimated that about 1.38 million people in rural areas and 3.5 million to 4.1 million in urban areas < (which has increased from about 3 million persons in 2007), are highly food insecure in 2008 (Kenya Food Security. "KFSSG's Long Rains Assessment Report," 2008"). In rural areas, it is noted that the worst affected areas are situated in the pastoral zones of Turkana, Mandera, Samburu, Baringo, Marsabit, Wajir, Moyale and Garissa; significant areas in the agro pastoral and the marginal agricultural livelihoods. This statistic includes 300,000 former and current internally displaced
persons (IDPs).

In the marginal agricultural cluster in the lowlands of Mwingi, Kitui, Makueni, Machakos, Mbeere, Tharaka, Malindi, Kwale, Kilifi, Laikipia and Tana River districts, about 80 percent of these areas have experienced a near total crop failure. Only some of the drought tolerant pigeon peas, sorghum and millet have survived. The food security has generated negative health consequences. For example, it is observed that the rates of stunting are over 30 percent, especially in the coastal Malindi, Kilifi and Kwale districts, indicative of an extended period of malnutrition.

In Kenya, the major causes of food insecurity often mentioned are the rain factor; the spread of *peste de petits ruminants* (PPR) livestock disease; heightened food and non-food prices; ethnic strife; inadequate coping strategies to deal with drought, floods and conflict; and decreasing cross-boarder trade and Strategic Grain Reserves (Kenya Food Security. "KFSSG's Long Rains Assessment Report," 2008"). Yet the most import problem, like other resource-poor countries, is the lack of infrastructure and capacity to support food security.

The post-election conflict that started in 27 December, 2007, has added fuel to an already unstable situation of food insecurity that spread across the Rift Valley, Western, Nyanza and Nairobi provinces and has affected the urban poor in particular (Reuters. "Post-election Conflict Causes Extreme Food Insecurity in Rural Areas, Urban Centers." January 2008). As a result of this crisis, it was estimated that more than 256,000 people had been displaced from their homes (Kenya Food Security. "KFSSG's Long Rains Assessment Report," 2008"). For the major staple of maize, the situation was serious because the maize from the Rift Valley highlands is the bread basket for the country. The crisis affected the harvest of about 20 percent of the maize at the onset of the crisis and impacted the purchases of the crop by the National Cereals and Produce Board (NCPB) (Kenya Food Security. "KFSSG's Long Rains Assessment Report," 2008"). The crisis also affected other food-related provisions, such as perishables (milk and vegetables), supply of gasoline, and food access services, such as the NPCB, milk delivery depots, grain milling and veterinary services (Reuters. "Post-election Conflict Causes Extreme Food Insecurity in Rural Areas, Urban Centers." January 2008.),

It was noted that conflict occurs between pastoralists in Wajir and Garissa has spilled into Sericho in the Isiolo District and the conflict between herders and crop growers in the Tana Delta resulted in displacements and reduced livestock production prospects. The other kind of conflict that is not un-common is the competition for grazing resources. The conflict could cause the closure of markets, inaccessibility of services, and loss of human life and stock.

As mentioned earlier, in Kenya, food security is gauged mainly by the supply of several crops. The major crop is maize, which accounts for 80 percent of total cereals, and thus the supply of maize plays a critical role in food security (FAO, "Special Report: Crop and Food Supply Situation in Kenya. 10 July, 2000). However, maize is also sensitive to local and global factors. For example, the global economic fluctuations and political instability have contributed to heightened prices of maize. The maize prices were 40 percent higher in 2008 than in 2007.

Other staples include rice, wheat, millet, and sorghum, and their pro-ductivity is related to such factors as the use of high-yielding seed varieties, fa-vorable agro-climatic conditions, hectarage; sustained high prices; adoption of optimal seed rates; improved soil testing that helps the use of appropriate fertil-izers; and intensification of extension services. Water availability, mainly from rain, is the most crucial factor in maize production.

In general, the root causes of food insecurity facing Kenya are not too different from those facing other resource-poor countries, and these causes are often interrelated. These are mainly related to the historical factors of the colo-nial practices of exclusion and misplaced development agenda, which has nega-tively affected the growth of community capital, especially human capital. These factors then lead to constant ethnic strife and political instability, a lack of infra-structure investment, water and land mismanagement, which then creates a vi-cious cycle of poverty and even weaker human capacity to tackle food insecu-rity.

In this case, a downstream, immediate solution would be to provide immediate relief. And it has been effectively applied by the Kenyan government and international relief agencies. For example, in 2008, the Kenya Red Cross appealed to the US aid of $15.4 million to provide a comprehensive package that addresses such needs as public health; water and sanitation; capacity building; security; food relief; non-food relief; and communications. This was joined by the Kenyan government's $7.5 million on-going relief effort. The country has planned to import maize from South Africa to cover the immediate inadequacy and prevent the shortage in 2009. Other donors, such as the United States Gov-ernment, DFID, the Australian Government, UN agencies and NGOs have also participated in the relief with a comprehensive package of interventions in health and nutrition; water and sanitation; agriculture and livestock; education; relief food; and peace-building (*Reuters.* "Post-election Conflict Causes Ex-treme Food Insecurity in Rural Areas, Urban Centers." January 2008; see also Kenya Food Security. "KFSSG's Long Rains Assessment Report," 2008").

Kenya's food insecurity situation should be part of the framework of global topstream solutions. In specific, in the case of Kenya, the goal should be *to improve governance, political stability and its sustainable development agenda as the overarching framework to improve food security.* The confrontation between the supporters of President-elect Mwai Kibaki and discontented Raila Odinga, who lost the election, is regarded as a combination of the long-standing problem of ethnic strife and the negative legacy of colonial practice of "divide and rule" the latter tending to enforce the existing ethnic division. Competition among the major powers for the sphere of influence in Africa during and after the colonial rule has weakened local community capital, especially in inequity and access to opportunities and resources. In Kenya, this inequity has deepened ethnic division because politics is perceived as an exercise of favoritism, usually by the ruling Kikuyu over other tribes, especially over Luo, the largest minority.

In this context, the wealth gap is a major social issue that worsens other inequities, including food security. According to the UN Office for the Coordination of Humanitarian Affairs, Kenya has one of the largest wealth gaps in the world, and 60 percent of the populations live in slums (IRIN. "Kenya. It's the Economy, Stupid." 9 January, 2008). Kenya is the tenth most unequal in wealth disparities in the world and is the fifth most unequal among the 54 African states (See IRIN, "Kenya. It's the Economy, Stupid," 9 January, 2008). It is also calculated that in Kenya, the top 10 percent of the population controls 42 percent of the country's wealth, while the bottom 10 percent own 0.76 percent (IRIN, "Kenya. It's the Economy, Stupid," 9 January, 2008). Disparities exist among different ethnic groups and are reflected not only in income distribution but also in access to education, water and health; life expectancy; and prevalence of HIV/AIDS. Despite the fact that the current president Kibak has been credited with the high-growth economy scenario in Kenya, it is widely perceived that the beneficiary is his own Kikuyu group and that this group dominates politics and the economy (IRIN, "Kenya. It's the Economy, Stupid," 9 January, 2008).

Since this challenge of governance and political stability is facing most of the post-colonial countries in Africa, improved governance and sustainable peace and stability should be on the top of the topstream solutions. Along the same line of thinking, former Secretary-General Kofi Annan made it clear that the fundamental solution is to address the current disparities because for a long time, global and local resources have not benefited those at the bottom of the population pyramid (*The Christian Science Monitor*, "Out of Kenya's Violence, Rebirth," 12 February, 2008). The specific measures to achieve sustainable stability are several. To start, Africa needs to build government's capacity in political inclusion. The root of Kenya's conflict is that the forty-two ethnic groups or tribes, other than the Kikuyus, feel excluded from the political process. As Kofi Annan suggested in his intervention, the fundamental solution would be shared governance, namely, political inclusion (*The Christian Science Monitor*, "Out of Kenya's Violence, Rebirth," 12 February, 2008). In this case, it was obvious that because its historical experience, Kenya has encountered a lot of difficulty in moving in that direction. The fact that Kofi Annan's intervention has worked showed that the post-colonial countries are in urgent need of capacity building to improve governance, especially in inclusion, transparency, and accountability. When an accountable government is in place, the leadership also needs to correct its development agenda that sustains its populace and its environment. Resources should be devoted to such sustainable goals as inclusive social cohesion and environmental integrity. In addition, the world can help the region by supporting the local peace-keeping capacities. There have been plans by the United States and EU and G-8 to improve their peace-keeping missions in the region. For example, G-8 supports an *Africa Action Plan* to improve the peace-keeping capacities in the region (Stimson Center. July, 2007*)*. Yet given the historical experience of the African countries with their colonizers, these plans could encounter resistance if there is an "impure" agenda of extending the former colonialists' hegemony on the continent. A community-centered approach would be to strengthen the capacity of the leading regional organizations, such as African Union (AU), the Economic Community of West African States, and SADC in their effective and efficient prevention of and intervention in regional conflicts. Under President Bush, there have been suggestions that the United States should build a regional military base in Africa. This is an intriguing proposal because this might convey the impression that the United States is extending its military control in Africa rather than addressing Africa's immediate problem of lacking stable governance and sustainable resources. Also, global powers need to exercise serious restraint in the weapon sales to the region to prevent the fueling of the ethnic strife.

Once the governance, peace and stability issue is addressed, the upstream solutions target food-related problems, with a focus on food self-sufficiency, and non-food preventions (Global Monitoring for Food Security, 2007, "Food Security"). With the goal of food self- sufficiency in the center of policy making, governments should address such interrelated issues as monitoring/early warning, agricultural mapping, yield assessment, water management (water demand forecasting, impact assessment of the long rains and short rains, water reserve and relief); land management; agricultural productivity and efficiency; technology; roads, transportation and distribution; storage and reserves; livestock issues (disease preventions and interventions, such as vaccinations); and financing and trade policies (national debt, difficulty in obtaining credit and aid, protectionism in developed countries). (See related discussions in Global Monitoring for Food Security, 2007, "Food Security").

These solutions should be embedded in a multi-sector and multi-lateral framework in building the mechanisms to ensure supply and demand/need balance (Kenya Food Security, "KFSSG's Long Rains Assessment Report," 2008").

Other non-food interventions include the establishment of a monitoring, forecasting and assessment system on prices; setting up price control mechanisms (for food and contributing factors); sustaining a long-term program of recovery (some form of food loans, food stamps, food for work etc.); and building household resilience (See some of the discussions in Kenya Food Security. "KFSSG's Long Rains Assessment Report," 2008").

Upstream solutions might vary from region to region because of the manifestation of different problems in different regions but the goal is similar, that is, to establish local technical capacities. In Kenya, different livelihood zones have different agricultural, geo-physical, socio-economic, and cultural characteristics. For example, the pastoral livelihood zone that covers Turkana, Marsabit, Moyale and Samburu districts is characterized by disproportionate dependence on livestock as the major source of food and income in a drought-prone environment and is one of the most food-insecure zones (ibid). Pastoralists obtain most of their cereals and other food commodities from the markets, thus making them highly vulnerable to food and non-food prices fluctuations. In addition, the pastoralists are also vulnerable to negative pasture and grazing conditions and local conflicts, which would force them engage in early or extended migrations that generate negative impact on livestock. There, food insecurity is indicated by the high rates of malnutrition; reduced food access and availability due to increase in commodity prices, livestock diseases, crop failure, poor dietary diversification, poor child care practices, inadequate clean water and poor hygiene and sanitation practices (the sanitation coverage in this region is less than a worrisome 30 percent) (The statistic derives from Kenya Food Security, "KFSSG's Long Rains Assessment Report," 2008").

It has been suggested that in this case, the major solution is to strengthen the resilience of pastoral livelihood in general and it requires very effective multi-sector partnerships (the suggestion derives from Kenya Food Security. "KFSSG's Long Rains Assessment Report," 2008"). Some of the specific measures suggested are improving water availability, such as water storage and rehabilitation of water sources (existing programs cover only 50 percent of the need); diversifying the local economies in the long term; increasing prevention and intervention of livestock diseases, such as PPR vaccination (because there is a 85 percent gap in the coverage of PPR vaccination); improving health and sanitation services (the current program covers only up to 70 percent); establishing food supplement programs, especially for pregnant women and children (the statistic on coverage of sanitation program derives from Kenya Food Security, "KFSSG's Long Rains Assessment Report," 2008").

Another agro pastoral livelihood zone, which includes Kajiado, Narok, West Pokot, Laikipia and Baringo Districts, also experiences food insecurity. In this livelihood zone, the major source of food is livestock, which accounts for over 50 percent of total household income, complemented by 30 percent of crop production. In this zone, the most serious food shortage is reported in the Baringo District, which has worsened considerably. The major factors of food insecurity in this zone are a combination of the disease PPR; poor rains; a near-total crop failure; high food prices and heightened conflict (These were mentioned in Kenya Food Security, "KFSSG's Long Rains Assessment Report," 2008").

Several measures have been in use in this zone. For example, there are interventions to increasing the value of agricultural produce and facilitate adequate storage at the household level; and provisions of drought-tolerant seed varieties; use of PPR, FMD (Foot and Mouth Disease) and CCPP (Pleuropneumonia) vaccination for an estimated 30-35 percent of the livestock; imposition of a quarantine against FMD and PPR infected livestock; supporting Comprehensive Care Clinics in Kajiado, West Pokot and Baringo; and increasing the use of distilling water pans and construction of boreholes. The major problem is that the scope of the interventions is still limited (See the information in Kenya Food Security, "KFSSG's Long Rains Assessment Report," 2008").

The other livelihood zone, the coastal marginal agricultural livelihood, shares a similar set of problems as the agro pastoral livelihood zone and is characterized by extremely high chronic food insecurity in several areas. Chronic factors include poor crop husbandry; increasing and unresolved wildlife-human conflict; a decline in the tourism sector; outbreaks of livestock diseases. Theses factors have contributed to poverty and extended periods of under-nutrition.

Some of the measures currently taken by the government and local communities are rehabilitation of water sources; provision of seeds for drought-tolerant crops; promotion of improved crop and livestock husbandry (upgrading goat breeds); increased access to water for households and schools; regular school feeding program; and the pilot school meals program in eight schools.

Overall, for the upstream solutions in these livelihood zones, it is important to obtain policy commitments to strengthen technical capacity and supply and demand/need infrastructure. For example, in the agro pastoral livelihood zone and coastal marginal agricultural livelihood zone, improvement of water supply is the key. Some possible measures are construction of sand and subsurface dams; construction of distilling public pans; rain water harvesting; drilling and equipping of new boreholes in appropriate locations; rehabilitation of water supplies and pipes and expansion of irrigation schemes; and improvement of sanitation and hygiene. The other critical factor is improvement in food production effectiveness and efficiency. For the pastoral region, some possible measures are improved livestock husbandry; livestock transportation and redistribution; creating new livestock businesses; diversifying economies; developing strategic feed reserves. For the agricultural region, possible measures are provision of assorted drought-tolerant crop seeds (cow peas, pigeon peas, and millet); improving soil conditions with sustainable methods (rotate farming, for example); provision of farming inputs, such as seed and fertilizer; provision of tools and animal traction equipment; establishing seed banks particularly in such vulnerable areas as marginal agricultural areas; provision of starter seed for planting; increasing agricultural activities in the marginal agricultural areas by promoting irrigated agriculture; improving land preparation efficiency by implementation of animal traction and other farming routines; provision of starter seed for planting; strengthening the capacity of pre-and post harvest management.

In terms of social protection mechanisms to strengthen community capital, the government can provide subsidies for food (food stamps, food for work programs, school meals, etc.) and non-food contributing factors (water, fuel, seeds, transportation, and storage). In terms of market linkages mechanisms, possible measures are some types of price protection mechanisms for produce and price-control mechanisms for food-contributing factors, such as seeds and fertilizers; improving roads and means of transportations; establishing direct sale mechanisms between breeders and retailers in the market; improved mechanisms of bartering. In terms of sustainable mechanisms, possible measures are strengthening policy designing, planning, and implantation in food security; providing permanent mechanisms to engage in community-based multi-sector partnerships to monitor food security situations.

Since the coastal marginal agricultural livelihood zone is a highly food non-secure region, especially after the 2007 elections, the downstream solutions need to be applied immediately and effectively to support recovery and livelihood resilience, and to control the high food prices.

On assessment, the inclusive partnership examines the success on the basis of the partnership (process) and the task (outcome) in both quantitative and qualitative manners. In this case, assessing the maintenance function involves examining if the partnerships for food insecurity has included all the key stakeholders, especially local pastoralists and farmers, beyond the intergovernmental agencies (the UN World Food Programme, the Red Cross, etc.), and Kenya Government. Some of the NGOs already involved in the local capacity building are the Kenya Food Security Steering Group (KFSSG), the National Council of NGOs of Kenya for Better Governance and Poverty Eradication, Building East African Community Network, the Children Legal Action Network, Corat Africa, Anppcan Kenya Chapter, Acacia Consultants Ltd, Amani Counseling Centre, Community Initiative Support, Helpage Kenya, the Consumer Information Network, Erastus & Company, African Women's Development, Iceberg Africa, the Institute of Cultural Affairs, the Kenya Institute of Management, the Population Council, the Kenya Polytechnic, Premese Africa Development, The Snow Mount Centre Strategic Dimensions, Technoserve, Tranforming Analysing, Private Sector Gorvernment, Winrock International, Community Based Livestock, Oxfam, Population Services, the World Health Organization, the Aga Khan Foundation Kenya, Africa Now, the United Nations Children's Fund, International Livestock Research, Maji na Ufanisi, the Kenya Human Rights Commission, Matrix Development Consultants, the Rockefeller Foundation, Action Aid, the Anglican Church of Kenya, Centre for In SOS Children Villages Kenya, digenous, K-rep Development Agency, World Neighbours EA Program, Care International in Kenya, and so on. These NGOs have worked to improve food-related issues; engage in advocacy and networking with other stakeholders for adoption of policies favorable to the livestock initiatives; empower marginalized people; and enhance political participation (The National Council of NGOs. "NGO Support Organizations." 2003). Therefore, including them is important for a food security partnership.

On assessing the partnership process, we can examine if the stakeholders share the risks and responsibilities in short-term and long-term objectives and goals and if the community representation is adequate. The partnership also examines the quality and quantity of communication and decision making process. Assessing the partnership process is critical because that is the only way that we can gain some information about whether these partners have gained additional skills in the process. The desired goal is that these local partners will bring the experience back to the community that increases local capacity building in tackling food insecurity.

On assessing the task, in this case, the partnership can assess the amount of food relief being delivered to the needy. For downstream solutions, we can assess the number of individuals on the relief programs. For upstream solutions, we can assess agricultural productivity, prices, nutritional intake and deficiency levels, health status (morbidity and mortality), progress in food-related infrastructure building, and community capacity at the population level. On topstream solutions, there are several areas that can be targeted, such as global policy progress, peace, governance, equity, and sustainability. For example, on sustainability, we can assess if food solutions have been integrated with other social policies. For example, we examine if there is a balance between macro and micro- agricultural policies (especially in the balance between cash crops and maintenance of small farms), global trade, food subsidies, environmental protection, energy use, harmonization of global development agenda, empowerment of women's participation in agricultural sector, quality education and skill updates, etc. We also need to assess if there is a long-term, follow-up and monitoring plan for the solutions to take root in the community. Most important of all, we need to examine if the capacities of the affected communities have been strengthened to achieve food self-sufficiency. The sustainable solutions are beyond short-term food relief and they require the topstream solutions on a globally harmonized platform at the multilateral and multi-sector levels. Sustainability should be the ultimate goal of global inclusive partnerships.

Energy

Energy security is close related to global peace, environmental integrity, and food security and it has serious implications on global health and development. For a long time, the crux of the problem has been a lack of stability in the supply and demand of energy. Or to be more specific, there is a lack of long-term vision in the global political leadership to support alternative, renewable energy that would gradually replace oil.

The concern about supply and demand/need imbalance in energy has been acute since the first oil crisis in the 1970s. However, the problem of energy insecurity has got worse. It was noted that since the early 2000s, global demand has been outpacing energy supply and the fight for the control of oil and gas has increased international tensions. Statistics show that since World War II, oil consumption has grown eightfold while gas consumption has grown at an even faster rate because the demand for both has contributed to global economic growth (Klare, "May 9, 2005). A forecast from the United States Department of Energy shows that by 2025, global oil consumption is likely to increase by 57 percent and gas consumption will grow by 68 percent, and these demands will not be met by the world's energy industry (Klare, May 9, 2005). And this demand comes from developed as well as the emerging industrialized countries, especially East Asia, India, Latin America, and Southeast Asia. China and India are likely to outpace other countries in the demand for oil. It is projected that between 2001 and 2025, China's oil consumption is estimated to increase by 156 percent and India's will increase by 152 percent (Klare, May 9, 2005). These days, the fight for control over energy has become a major cause of international tensions. For example, the fight for the right of gas drilling in a disputed area of the East China Sea has caused the vociferous diplomatic war between Japan and China (Klare, May 9, 2005). In April, 2005, India's plan to import natural gas from Iran had caused grave concerns from the United States, when the United States was trying to impose international sanctions on Iran. The fact that Iran has some control over oil supply has long been a concern in the West. The dispute between Iran and Azerbaijan, an ally of the United States, concerning control over offshore oil and gas fields, caused a gunboat conflict in 2001 (Klare, May 9, 2005). To protect its own interests in the region, the United States has established a plan to build a "Caspian Guard," a network of police forces and special-operations units to respond to assaults on its oil facilities. A similar move is planned by the Russian fleet (See_Fialka, "Search for Crude Comes With New Dangers," 11 April, 2005). At the height of rising oil prices, the rapprochement by Russia and Chavez of Venezuela has raised concerns in the West because both countries have rich energy reserves. It is also worth noting that all the major oil-producing countries, such as Iran, Iraq, Kuwait, Nigeria, Russia, and Venezuela, have major political or geopolitical disputes with their neighboring countries or with the Western countries that could affect the supply of oil in the rest of world.

Applying the inclusive sustainable development theory, the solution framework for energy insecurity is similar to that for global food security. In a nutshell, the goal of downstream solutions is to meet immediate energy needs to sustain livelihood and resolve energy-related conflicts. Possible measures are providing immediate energy relief (discounts or coupons) for cooking or heating for displaced populations (refugees, and victims of conflict and disasters) and resource-poor populations (the chronically poor, homeless, the elderly, etc.); promoting energy saving measures that can be immediately put into practice (such as day-light saving time; lowering heater temperatures during winter; etc.). Upstream solutions are mid-term energy-efficient measures. Possible measures are generating policies and tax incentives for energy efficiency in every aspect of social life (such as improved insulation, solar panels, production of efficient vehicle, encouraging the use of public transportation, and production of clean and efficient bio-fuel; increasing use of alternative energy that is currently available); disincentives (increasing gasoline tax); and capacity building for renewable energy (increasing the public support for the R&D of renewable energy; increasing tax incentives for the innovative technology for renewable energy produced by the private sector; and increasing incentives for the public use of renewable energy). Topstream solutions aim for sustainable energy use and the most important step in this area would be to reach a global consensus in energy saving and the development of renewable energy. Most important of all, the global leaders need to correct the "winnership" model of development, based on competition and limitless consumption. This model has generated more negatives than positives for development, such as unreasonable, excessive wealth gaps, increasing conflicts, environmental degradation, and health disparities that hamper the long-term prospect of human development.

Therefore, the core of the topstream solutions is to generate a different conceptual framework of our development agenda because it would affect energy use in a most direct and profound way. This would require the global community to generate a collaboration policy platform that supports energy saving and increasing use of sustainable energy (such as solar energy, wind, geothermal, etc.).

This partnership for energy security would involve almost every sector of the global community, such as the United Nations, governments, the private sector, the scientific community, civil society, populations, etc. And the economic benefits of the partnership could be enormous because according to an estimate by Credit Suisse, wind and solar industries that currently form about 7 percent of the total renewable energy market are expected to rise to more than 25 percent of renewable energy by 2030 (Environment Leader, 5 February, 2009).

In this case, leadership matters, but multi-sector support is also indispensable. For example, in Germany, the environmentally conscious public lends strong support for government's green policies to encourage renewable energies, and today, Germany is a leader in the renewable energy and this effort has also benefited its economy. It is estimated that In 2008, about 7.3 percent of Germany's primary energy consumption is based on the renewables, but this figure is likely to increase to 33 percent by 2020 and if the political leadership accelerates this effort, Germany could be the world's first industrial power to use 100 percent renewable energy (See Burgermeister, 3 April, 2009). This effort could add about 800,000 to 900,000 new clean tech jobs for Germany by 2030 (Burgermeister, 3 April, 2009). In China, in the spring of 2009, the government's decisions to subsidize the nationwide use of solar energy and encourage the use of electric batteries for automobiles will also have a profound impact on the future of energy security in China as well as the world. On 26 March, 2009, China's Ministry of Finance announced a program immediately in effect for a subsidy of 20 RMB/watt, or about $3, for large solar installations and according to an estimate, this subsidy is tantamount to about a 60 percent subsidy for upfront cost (Barron's, 26 March, 2009). In this respect, the United States also embodies tremendous potential. A report shows that by April, 2009 the US has overtaken Germany to become a leader in wind-generated energy, with an increased wind-generation capacity of 50 percent compared with last year (White and Graham, 2 February, 2009).

In summary, this chapter has demonstrated the use of the inclusive sustainable development theoretical framework to the analysis of food and energy security challenges facing the world today. This analysis shows that there need different types of solutions targeting different problems at different stages and for solutions to be sustainable, the global community has to work in partnerships for generating topstream, upstream, and downstream solutions. In addition to food and energy security, the most critical element of sustainable development is water security. Water security is the mother of sustainable development and is facing the most serious challenge today. The story of water insecurity will be discussed in the final chapter of this book.

Chapter 4

Africa: Cornerstone of Sustainable Health and Development: Global Water Security

Since the beginning of the twenty-first century, most of the development challenges seem to have converged to create a formidable force unseen in human history. This force seems to be moving in such velocity that it could forestall the progress and growth of humanity. The outbreaks of natural disasters and epidemics and pandemics have been worsened by human-made crises in the financial sector, environmental degradation, water, food, energy, and clean air insecurity, internecine and international conflict, wealth gaps, health disparities and so on. There is not one country or one group that can be singled out for blame. Yet it is clear that our worst enemy is the negative development consequences of our own making. And what is most worrisome is our inability to generate creative and effective solutions tackling the root causes of these problems. In the face of these challenges, some short-term solutions have been used but there still lacks a long-term plan to address these issues. In fact, the roots of the problems were not planted just days ago. They have been in the making for hundreds of years, and despite some progress in certain areas of global lives, humanity measures poorly in terms of sustainable development outcomes and for a long time, the dominant model of thinking about development and economy has brought about negative consequences for the resource-poor populations.

Today, sustainable development challenges have become major threats to humanity. These threats are most obvious in our access to the fundamental elements of life, such as clean air, water, food, and energy. These threats in turn pose a danger to our pursuit of equitable and peaceful social lives (in which all have equitable access to resources, rights and opportunities). Among all these challenges, the environmental breakdown has aroused most attention because environment is the mother of all the fundamental elements of life and the source of survival for human beings and other species. One of the most valid indicators of environmental problems is the extent of water insecurity and it is no exaggeration to say that water is the most critical element in global health and sustainable development.

The case of water security deserves scrutiny because it has multiplying effects on other areas of development, such as food and energy security, population health, industry, tourism, etc. Water-related issues have a particularly serious effect on those populations whose livelihood depends on the adequacy of water, such as in farming or in fishing or energy generation. The purpose of this chapter is to apply the architectural framework of the inclusive sustainable development theory to the analysis of water security. In the end, the solutions to water challenges illustrate the interconnectedness of development problems and the need to resolve these problems in an inclusive and sustainable manner. And the solutions for water challenges have a profound impact on the future of sustainable development.

Water

The supply and demand imbalance of water has caused global water insecurity. Water insecurity pertains to the lack of access to clean, usable and/or potable drinking water and the insecurity is mainly related to population growth, urbanization, industrialization, and growing water demand from agriculture (See Webb and Iskandarani, 1998). Overall, water insecurity has generated several risks to human beings. These are 1. lacking access to water for drinking and sanitation, which leads to the prevalence of water-borne illnesses and diseases, such as cholera; 2. unstable supply of water for agricultural production that threatens food security; 3. contamination of water because of an increase of conventional and non-conventional toxic pollutants, and life-threatening bacterial contamination; 4. threats to water resources and ecosystems; 5. transboundary water conflicts because of a lack of global framework governing the sharing of water resources; and 6. aggravation of water insecurity because of privatization of water service in the global trade framework.

Water Supply and Demand Imbalance

An estimate based on the population of 2000 shows that theoretically, there is almost sufficient water, or some 34,000 cubic kilometers, available for human use annually in the world. In this estimate, each person has about 8,000 cubic meters of water at his/her disposal if water resources are evenly distributed. In other words, ideally, every person should have enough water to meet basic needs (Hinrichsen, (2008); see also Acreman. "2008). However, this estimate is affected by several intervening factors. First, water withdrawals are increasing while water supply is unstable and is decreasing in some cases. On the side of water supply, waterstocks have fallen from 1700 cubic meters per person per year in the 1980s to 907 in 2007 and by 2050, water availability will be for 420 per person per year by 2050 (Oliver, 18 December, 2007). It was also noted that between 1950 and 1980, water availability declined by 40 percent in Asia and 50 percent in Africa (See Ayibotele, 1992). On the side of demand, according to the United Nations, the demand for water by developing countries will increase by more than 50 percent by 2025 (Oliver, 18 December, 2007). In another estimate, overall water withdrawals are expected to increase by 35 percent by 2020. While the rate of demand is rising faster in developing countries, the populations in developed countries consume larger share per capita than their counterparts in developing countries (See Webb and Iskandarani, 1998; see also Rosengrant, 1995). Pollution also aggravates water availability. One estimate shows that more than half of the world's major rivers are polluted and/or drying up in the downstream because of overuse (International Relations and Security Network (IRIN), "A Thirsty World." 2009). In addition, water resources are not evenly distributed throughout the planet. One report shows that nine countries (Brazil, Russia, Canada, Indonesia, China, Colombia, the US, Peru, and India.) hold 60 percent of the world's water resources. In contrast, many others rely significantly on water resources outside their national borders, for example, Turkmenistan's 96 percent, Egypt's 96 percent, and Syria's 84 percent) (International Relations and Security Network, 2009). And about 33 countries depend on other countries for more than fifty percent of their renewable water resources (International Relations and Security Network, 2009). It was noted that the Congo River supplies about 30 percent of the water resources in Africa, while only 10 percent of Africa's population lives in its watershed (Hinrichsen, 2008). There are also very large disparities in per capita share of water. Theoretically, a minimum of 500 cubic meters of water per capita per year is the lowest standard for global populations. However, the actual availability per capita varies from country to country and within a country, from region to region. In China, most of the rivers and lakes are concentrated in the southeast part of the country, while the population in the northwest face water scarcity every day. In the United States, on average, each American has 8,838 cubic meters of water at his/her disposal per person per year but those in the Colorado River Basin have only slightly over 2,000 cubic meters per person per year, and those in the Rio Grande River Basin have less than 620 cubic meters per person per year (WWF International. "World's Top 10 Rivers at Risk," March, 2007). The water shortage is also felt in other arid areas in the United States (See Webb, Patrick and Maria Iskandarani, 1998). This water inequity is also reflected in the access to rainfall, the major source of water for populations in developing countries. Overall, two-thirds of the population in the world has access to only a quarter of the rainfall (Commonwealth Parliamentary Conference. "Access to Water in Developing Countries." 2007). And most of the rainfall tends to occur in only few months during a year, such as the short monsoon season in South Asia and Southeast Asia (See Encyclopedia Britannica. "Monsoon." 2009).

Second, the other intervening factor is the multiple-function use of water and undesirable effect of water pollution. Water today is not just for meeting basic human needs of drinking and bathing or other household use. It is a "blue gold" that has multiple derivative values. Water is used to meet many needs of human life, such as irrigation in agriculture and fish farming, energy, industry, and environmental cleanup. Unfortunately, a major product of these processes is pollution. Almost all of our water sources are polluted. For example, about 97 percent of the world's population relies on ground water while almost all the ground water on every inhabited continent is polluted (Oliver, 2007). World-wide, it was estimated that about 450 cubic kilometers of wastewater are dis-charged into rivers, streams and lakes annually. To clean up for re-use requires about 6,000 cubic kilometers of clean water, or two-thirds of global total usable fresh water (Hinrichsen, 2008). Another estimate by the UNESCO shows that about 500 million tons of heavy metals, solvents, and toxic sludge are dumped into global water supply every year and about 70 percent of untreated industrial waste is dumped into rivers and lakes (Oliver, 2007). The other source of pollu-tion is agricultural runoff that contains nutrients and agrochemicals, such as ni-trates, pesticides, biosolids or sewage sludge being the source of such excessive nutrients as phosphorus. These nutrients acclerate eutrophication and reduced oxygen in the water (Oliver, 2007). Water pollution is an especially serious problem in the populous developing countries, such as India and China (Pacific Environment, "Water Pollution in China." 2009). One report shows that 70 per-cent of China's rivers and lakes are polluted (Pacific Environment, 2009). In India, about 80 percent of the urban waste is dumped into the nation's river sys-tem and just in Delhi alone, 55 percent of the residents are not connected to a sewage system (Spiegel Online. July, 2007). The untreated sewage is the major culprit of India's pollution problem and a report showed that samples from the Ganges River near Varanasi indicated that levels of fecal coliform, a dangerous bacterium from untreated sewage, were some 3,000 percent higher than the safety standard for bathing water (Spiegel Online, July, 2007). However, water pollution is not just a problem in the developing countries. According to an es-timate, in the United States, about 60 percent of the most toxic liquid is dumped into groundwater and about 40 percent of estuaries suffer from severe eutrophi-cation and 14 million people regularly drink water contaminated with carcino-genic chemicals (Oliver, 2007).

Third, another compounding factor that affects water availability is ex-ponential population growth and rapid urbanization in most developing coun-tries, which deepens pollution and makes it even more difficult for the resource-poor populations to access water.

Major indicators show that water insecurity is worsening from year to year. Water stress is experienced when annual water supplies drop below 1,700 cubic meters per person, and a country faces water scarcity for part or all of the year when annual water supplies fall below 1,000 cubic meters per person per year (Hinrichsen, 2008). According to this measure, a large number of people in the world is already facing water insecurity. For example, in 1995, it was esti-mated that 31 countries, or the total of a billion people, have regularly faced either water stress or water scarcity, and this number will increase to 48 coun-tries containing about 3 billion people in 2025; and to 54 countries and 4 billion people, or 40 per cent of the projected world population of 9.4 billion, in 2050. It was observed that the situation has worsened since 2000. United Nations En-vironment Programme, in its Global International Waters Assessment in 2006, estimates that by 2025, 1.8 billion people will face acute water scarcity, while two-thirds of humanity (over 5 billion) will face water stress (shortages for all or part of the year) (United Nations Development Programme. "Action on Water." 2006). The World Resources Institute, which examines water availability in relation to population pressures by the measure of river basin, shows that currently 2.3 billion people, or 41 per cent of the world's population, live in water-stressed areas (World Resource, 2007). In this estimate, about 1.7 billion live in water-scarce areas, accessing less than 1,000 cubic meters per person per year (World Resource, 2007).

The worst situation of water insecurity is found in the 20 countries in the Near East and North Africa, and this region is likely to witness the slow depletion of water in the long term (Info For Health. "The Coming Era of Water Stress and Scarcity." 1998). It was observed that since 1972, the demand of water from its rivers and aquifers has exceeded the supplies every year. The worst cases of Jordan and Yemen were cited to show that they withdraw 30 per cent more water from groundwater annually than is replenished, followed by Israel's 15 per cent (Hinrichsen, 2008). It is believed that this excessive demand is likely to lead to falling water tables and drying aquifers (Hinrichsen, 2008; see also Info For Health, "The Coming Era of Water Stress and Scarcity," 1998). Even in the United States, it is estimated that groundwater reserves are being overused in many areas because the rate of usage is 25 percent greater than its replenishment rate (Info For Health. "The Coming Era of Water Stress and Scarcity." 1998). This rate of depletion is even faster in the western part of the country. For example, the extensive Ogallala aquifer, which extends parts of six states and irrigates 6 million hectares, is noted to have been overly used (Info For Health. "The Coming Era of Water Stress and Scarcity." 1998).

Water crisis is acutely felt in the developing countries experiencing rapid industrialization. For example, it was noted that China, with 22 percent of the world's population, has at its disposal only 7 percent of the total of the world's freshwater run-off (Wikinvest. "China's Water Scarcity." 2009). Another estimate shows that in China 39 percent of its rivers and 75 percent of its lakes are polluted heavily (Wikinvest. "China's Water Scarcity." 2009). The water situation in China is another case of a supply-demand imbalance. In one estimate, China's freshwater supplies can support only half the country's population on a sustainable basis, and the shortage is acutely felt in northern China(Wikinvest. "China's Water Scarcity." 2009).

It was noted that since 2000, about 67 percent, or 400, of China's cities, including Beijing, have suffered from water shortages (Wikinvest. "China's Water Scarcity." 2009).. Among them, about one hundred and ten cities are facing severe shortages. This trend has implications for China's long-term development (See Wikinvest, 2009). This dilemma is also felt in the megacities in other developing countries, such as in Bangkok, Dhaka, Jakarta, Lagos, Manila, and New Delhi (Hinrichsen. 2008). The water-related challenges will be particularly severe in megacities because according to UNESCO, most of the population growth between 2010 and 2030 will be concentrated in cities and it will make water availability even more difficult for resource-poor populations (UNESCO. "One Size does not Fit All," 2008).

Causes

The culprit linked to water insecurity is the conflicting goals of development at every level of global governance which creates a severe imbalance of supply and demand. The pressure for developing countries to pursue a "high-consumption" and "high-growth" model of economy pits water needs of some sectors against those of other sectors and this could have a negative, long-term impact on water resources.

Water Problems

Today, water problems have manifested themselves in many aspects of global lives. WHO and UNICEF estimate that 2.6 billion people have little access to acceptable means of sanitation and that more than 1.2 billion people have no access to clean, piped water (see World Water Council, "Water Supply and Sanitation, 2008; see also Hinrichsen, 2008).

According to the World Bank, about 88 percent of all diseases are cased by unsafe drinking water, inadequate sanitation, and poor hygiene practices (Oliver, 2007). Water related problems are causing 4 billion cases of diarrhea, which cause the deaths of 6 million children every year; 300 million cases of malaria; 200 million cases of shistosomiasis; 6 million cases of blindness by trachoma, and 500 million cases at risk of contracting trachoma (Oliver, 2007). Unsanitary water is also the cause of 1.5 million cases of hepatitis A and 133 million of intestinal worms (Oliver, 18 December, 2007). It is also estimated that at any one point in time, about half of all people in the developing world are affected by water-related problems (Oliver, 2007). Most of the affected will be children and water-related illness is the second largest killer of children worldwide (Oliver, 2007). Unfortunately, most of these water-related problems are preventable with access to safe water, adequate sanitation and hygiene.

In most developing countries, water shortage directly affects day-to-day subsistence. For example, in Kenya, lack of irrigation and rain stability causes food insecurity. Most of the agriculture in Kenya is rain-fed and only 3.5 percent of the agriculture uses irrigation (Encyclopedia of Earth, "Water Profile of Kenya," 2008). This heavy reliance on rainwater because of a lack of irrigation infrastructure has been a major contributing factor to Kenya's food insecurity. Periodic droughts become a major cause of this food insecurity. It was estimated that in the arid and semi-arid areas, about 2 million people are constantly threatened by water shortages and receive famine relief. When droughts occur, the population that needs relief rises to 5 million (Encyclopedia of Earth, "Water Profile of Kenya," 2008).

In international relations, water shortage has also brought about domestic and regional conflict. In China, there are daily conflicts between factories and farmers over resource and land-related issues (See Gleick, 2009; *Asia News Net*, "Sixty Thousand People Protest Against Pollution." 15 April, 2005). Water-related tensions are also experienced in other regions, such as the Middle East, Northern Africa, South Asia (India, Pakistan, and Bangladesh, or among the industrialized countries (such as Belgium, Poland, and the United States) (See

Water Is Life, 2004; see also Hinrichsen. 2008). In the United States, competition for water resources has long been a point of conflict between the American Indians and settlers (See Burton, 1991).

Water shortage threatens the health of our ecosystem because of its negative impact on species diversity and food chain integrity (Sustainability, January 2009). It is noted that all ecosystems require water to maintain their health as well as the health of the associated communities of plants, animals, and other living organisms (United Nations Environment Programme. "Fresh Water Under Threat: South Asia. 2008). In other words, there is a symbiotic relationship between fresh water and the wetlands ecosystem. In addition to its household, commercial, transportation, aesthetic, and recreational functions for human being, fresh water plays a major role in sustaining marshes, rivers, and coastal wetlands, which shelter millions of species (HARC, 15 September, 2006). In return, healthy natural ecosystems are natural regulators of water quality and quantity (Info For Health. "Consequences of Overuse and Pollution." 1998). Wetlands function as a natural flood regulator or a buffer to the damages of floods by soaking up, storing water, and reducing downstream damage. This "flow retardation" function is critical to contain floods (Kusler, 2008). And the global economic value of the wetland ecosystems functioning as flood regulators, waste treatment plants, and wildlife habitats, fisheries production and recreation, is estimated to be more than $5 trillion (See related discussions in Hinrichsen, 2008; see also RAMSAR, May 2003).

Humanity has now created a situation that pits our water needs not only against those of our fellow human beings but also against those of other species and therefore affects the health of this wetland ecosystem. In one estimate, the world's 6.7 billion people are now using over half of all the accessible freshwater contained in rivers, lakes, and underground aquifers. A conservative estimate shows that by 2025 humankind's share will be at least 70 per cent, if we take into account only the population growth factor. Yet if water use continues at its current rate, humanity will be appropriating 90 per cent of all available freshwater by 2025, leaving little for other species (Statistics cited from Hinrichsen, 2008).

The excessive demand from human beings leaves less and less for the maintenance of the vital wetland ecosystems. It was estimated that over 20 per cent of the approximately 10,000 freshwater fish species in the world are facing extinction and a significant percentage of mussels, amphibians, aquatic insects and other species are at risk (World Watch Institute, 2002). In China, the Yellow River, the major water supply in the northern China, is experiencing such excessive use that it was estimated that for an average of 70 days a year for the past decade, its waters dry up before reaching to the destination, Bohai Sea. And because of water shortage, the city of Beijing is experiencing intense water tensions with neighboring districts (Gleick, 2009).The farming delta, which is rapidly withering, has to compete with the upstream polluting factories and farms for water use. (Hinrichsen, 2008).

Water pollution merits special attention and immediate solutions in the world. As mentioned earlier, water pollution worsens environmental degradation. Human activities contaminate water bodies such as lakes, rivers, oceans, and groundwater. This contamination causes negative consequences in our ecosystem that affects the health of living organisms and plants (See Wikipedia. "Water Pollution." 2008).

The cases of China and India demonstrate that pollutants, especially from heavy and chemical industries, mining, and pharmaceutical productions, have aggravated the existing problem of water shortage. The World Bank forecasts that by 2020 there will be 30 million environmental refugees in China due to water problems (see Wikipedia. "China Water Crisis," 2009). Several facts are relevant: As mentioned earlier, China has more than 20 percent of the world's population but shares only 7 percent of the global water resources; more than half of China's 660 cities suffer from water shortages, affecting 160 million people; the per capita water volume in China is one-fourth of the world average; 90 percent of city groundwater and 75 percent of rivers and lakes are polluted; 700 million people drink contaminated water every day; waterborne diseases have created a rising number of premature deaths. In China, industrial waste has become a major risk factor in population health. The pollutants have also infiltrated the food chain and have become a risk factor for food safety. Greenpeace (2008) noted that China's industrial sector dumps an astonishing 40 to 60 billion tons of untreated wastewater into rivers and lakes every year, leaving little more than a precious 40 percent of water clean enough for drinking (Greenpeace, "Water Pollution Has Become China's Most Urgent Environmental Problem Today," 2008). It is believed that 90 million people in China are directly exposed to water pollution on a daily basis. Water for daily use is often contaminated with toxic substances, exceeding international safety standards (See Greenpeace, "Water Pollution Has Become China's Most Urgent Environmental Problem Today," 2008; see also Pacific Environment. "China Program." 2008). An estimate, citing the World Health Organization, also showed that nearly 100,000 Chinese die annually from water pollution-related illnesses, and 75 percent of disease comes from water quality issues (Pacific Environment. "China Program." 2008). The reports about the growing cancer rate in the so-called "cancer villages" near polluted water sources also show that water pollution might have caused a much more serious impact than what current data have revealed (Gleick, 2009).

In the United States, in addition to the widely known facts about industrial pollution, pharmaceutical contaminated water is a growing concern. It was noted that personal care products (PPCPs) and endocrine disrupting chemicals (EDCs) have been found in rivers, lakes, and groundwater, the major sources of drinking water, and even in treated drinking water. PPCPS include "over-the-counter (OTC) medications, prescription medications, dietary supplements, hormones, cleaning agents (especially antibacterial cleaners), and the inert ingredients associated with these products (which are believed to be just as harmful as the active ingredients themselves (Public Employees for Environmental

Responsibility (PEER), 2008). It was noted that many of the PPCPs are actually designed to impact the human hormone system. Some PPCPs containing Endocrine Disrupting Chemicals (EDCs), synthetic chemicals which either block or mimic natural hormones, might disrupt normal functioning of organs. The most commonly found EDC compounds in the United States were steroids, OTC medications (like ibuprofen), and insect repellants (Public Employees for Environmental Responsibility (PEER), 2008).

In India, pharmaceutical contamination is believed to be at the highest level compared to other countries. In 2008, a report by the Associated Press showed that pharmaceutical contamination was found in drinking water for at least 46 million Americans and concentrations of pharmaceuticals were found in all the rivers, lakes and streams. Yet in comparison, an analysis of the wastewater downstream from the Indian pharmaceutical plants showed that the contamination level was 150 times higher than those detected in the United States. The study by Joakim Larsson, an environmental scientist at the University of Gothenburg in Sweden, showed that the antibiotic Ciprofloxacin and the popular antihistamine cetirizine had the highest levels in the wells of six villages tested. In India, high levels of drug concentration were also found near pharmaceutical treatment plant (Mason, 25 January, 2009). http://www.americanchronicle. com/articles/yb/125760099).

Research suggests that pharmaceutical-contaminated water might lead to increasing drug resistance, which might inadvertently help the creation of "super bugs" and abnormal development of living organisms that would threaten ecological health (PEER, 2008).

In developing countries like Zimbabwe, contaminated water has triggered a major public health crisis. In Zimbabwe, the governance problem has caused decreased capacity in wastewater treatment and the lack of treatment has contributed to the cholera epidemic. It was reported that in the context of an ill-functioning government and an annual inflation rate of 231,000,000 percent, more than 11,000 people have infected with cholera, including more than 400 deaths, between August and December, 2008 (BBC. "'No water' in Cholera-hit Harare." 1 December, 2008). The major cause was the breakdown of the infrastructure, especially the inadequate water treatment system, which might have allowed human feces deposited in open spaces along the Mukuvisi River to infiltrate the public water supply, carrying the bacteria that causes cholera (See Voice of America. "Zimbabwe Cholera Crisis Mounts As Harare Water System Shut Down." 1 December, 2008; see also NPR, "Zimbabwe Cholera Tied To Crumbling Infrastructure," 2008).

In South America, a decrease of fresh water resource and increasing water pollution in the mining regions are a serious concern to the global community. It was noted that Andean glaciers, one of the Earth's important sources of freshwater, have experienced a sharp decline because of global warming. In 2006, the proposed gold mining project by Barrick Gold in the the Pascua-Lama site on the Argentine-Chilean border, which covers the extensive glaciers of Toro 1, Toro 2 and Esperan, caused a global protest. The water from the glaciers is the main source of irrigation for the Huasco Valley. Water contamination from mining is likely to affect the production of olives, grapes and vegetables. According to economist Marcel Claude of the international environmental group Oceana, "Gold mining dumps 79 tonnes of waste for every 28 grams of gold, and produces 96 percent of the world's arsenic emissions" (González, 2005).

Over the years, contaminated water from mining has caused serious health problems for the indigenous (See Guardian, "The Problem of Mining in the Andes? You Have to Move Glaciers." 3 May, 2006). A UN document indicates:

> "Indigenous communities tend to be exposed
> disproportionately to environmental degradation, in
> particular the contamination of water supplies by mine
> tailings, chemicals used by miners and pulp-and-paper
> mills, herbicides and pesticides used in agriculture and
> silviculture, and untreated sewage and trash from
> encroaching settlements. They are especially at risk
> because they not only lack the legal means to block
> destructive industrial activities, but lack the financial
> resources to install remedial environmental measures
> such as water purification and filtration facilities.
> Exposure to contaminants has direct impacts on
> health, causing death or, more often, chronic illness
> and disability. Contaminants also further weaken
> peoples' resistance to infection, and in this way
> aggravate the adverse consequences of malnutrition"
> (United Nations Economic and Social Council.
> COMMISSION ON HUMAN RIGHTS Sub-Commission
> on Prevention of Discrimination and Protection of
> Minorities Working Group on Indigenous Populations,
> 12 June, 1996).

Solutions

Applying the architecture of sustainable development, the goal is to improve the supply and demand balance of water management in the short term and the long term. First, in the cases of acute water scarcity or wide-spread epidemics, downstream solutions should be provided, such as the use of water storage devices (such as provision of clean water, boreholes, community reservoir) or purification devices (e.g., bio-sand) to prevent water-borne illnesses (cholera and diarrhea).

Second, for upstream solutions, there needs to be local capacity building for regulating the sources of water pollution; improving access to clean and usable water; water storage, and waste water management, such as through the use of water pipes, water filter tanks; and low-cost on-site treatment and waste recycling systems.

Third, topstream solutions should target root causes of water insecurity, such as unsustainable economic development programs, environmental degradation/climate change, global conflict, overpopulation, etc. The major action should focus on setting up and implementing policies for sustainable development at every level of global governance. These include building a global consensus on solutions to water problems. Unlike most other natural resources, water has transboundary implications. It has been pointed out that more than 200 major river systems cross international borders, and therefore it is urgent for international agreements to regulate the sharing of water resources. (Hinrichsen, 2008).

In practice, the international actions in sharing water resources will not be possible without multi-sector and community-based partnerships. In terms of the maintenance/process of partnership formation, the partnership should be based on a community-based participatory approach, involving users, planners and policy-makers; use of gender-sensitive approach (because of women's role in the provision, management and safeguarding of water and food security in most of the resource-poor regions); and aiming for community-initiated change. In terms of task, the partnerships would improve water governance structure; apply integrated water resources management for cross-border water management; coordinate and balance different water uses, such as water for food security, environment, energy, industry, transport, and tourism. For newly industrialized developing countries, there needs special attention for capacity building in processing wastewater with high concentrations of conventional pollutants (e.g oil and grease), toxic pollutants (e.g. heavy metals, volatile organic compounds) or other nonconventional pollutants such as ammonia.

Overall, the most important first step is to generate a global consensus for a concerted action platform, but currently there is no international agreement that provides a comprehensive framework for water use and preservation except some regional agreements. The 1997 Watercourses Convention, which was designed to provide a global legal framework to manage the water resources shared by different countries, has not been put into effect. The 1997 Convention was a good first step but in the face of the global water crisis, the world needs a much more comprehensive framework to address every aspect of the water crisis.

The hope of improving the topstream solutions might come from the existing regional efforts. For example, in November, 1999, the northern African states, including Egypt, Ethiopia, and Sudan, the region that suffers the worst water shortage, agreed upon a sustainable development strategy for equitable exploration of the Nile that benefits all the river basin states. The agreement is comprehensive in regulating the uses of the river, ranging from irrigation, hydropower, drainage, drought and flood control, to pollution prevention. (Hinrichsen, 2008).

In addition, a number of countries are already in the process of improving their policy and capacity framework for managing water resources (lakes and aquifers) and usage (in irrigation, industries, energy and household needs) but technical and financial support is urgently needed. In these countries, what is lacking is a central authority and comprehensive framework for prevention and intervention of water problems. Most of the resource-poor countries lack the organizational capacity for this undertaking. For example, in China, water issues are managed by several agencies. Water resources are monitored by the Ministry of Water Resources of the People's Republic of China, but related problems are managed by other authorities. Water pollution is managed by environmental agencies; sewage is tackled by the Ministry of Construction; and oversight of groundwater falls within the realm of the Ministry of Land and Resources (See Gleik, 2009; also Wikipedia, "Ministry of Water," 2008).

Other efforts in resource-poor settings are worth noting despite their imperfections. For example, Kenya has established a centralized structure and community partnership in water management. In Kenya, as a result of the Water Act 2002, the overall responsibility for water management lies with the Ministry of Water Resources Management and Development (MWRMD). Since 1999, its policy focuses on decentralization, privatization, commercialization, and stakeholder participation. Under Water Act 2002, the Water Resources Management Authority is in place to monitor water pollution, the management of lakes, aquifers, and rivers, and a Water Services Regulatory Board is responsible for water supply through licensed water services providers (Encyclopedia of Earth. "Water Profile of Kenya." 2008). Irrigation is managed by a number of institutions in the public and private sector. Under MWRMD, the National Irrigation Board (NIB) is in charge of developing the national irrigation schemes, and the Irrigation and Drainage Department (IDD) supports smallholder irrigation in a wide network across the country. Under the Ministry of Regional Development, the River Basin Development Authorities (RBDA) is in charge of the planning and use of the water and land resources within their jurisdiction.

The uniqueness of Kenya's system is the public-private partnerships between government institutions and non-governmental organizations in supporting irrigation development. Kenya's other strength is the community participation in the use of water resources. The multi-sector effort promotes the formation of water users associations (WUA) and communities own most of the structures and water rights for the irrigation scheme. Water users associations (WUA), which manage water resources issues within the smallholder irrigation schemes, address water issues at the local level.

Overall, it is clear that the major issue central to the water challenge is the diverse water needs for different development programs and the lack of adequate policies and legislation capacity to manage these needs. In China, as mentioned earlier, all the major water problems are related to the growing emphasis on industry as a major source of economy. This emphasis has caused serious water contamination and pollution and has reduced availability of clean and usable water for agriculture. For now, the government is accelerating its regulatory efforts. In the years to come, it will require coordinated effort to repair serious damages that have occurred. In Kenya, the major water challenges are related to inadequate capacities to address the water need of food production activities and, like China, to balance water needs for different social activities and programs. For example, irrigation, drainage, and water use for agriculture is hampered by the lack of a coherent national irrigation policy and implementation plan, which results in haphazard irrigation development with limited coordination among the various institutions. This also causes farmers' over-reliance on rainfall for agriculture, which puts considerable strains on its food security (Encyclopedia of Earth. "Water Profile of Kenya," 2008).

In Kenya, the irrigation act of 1966 is the only existing legal framework for the establishment of the NIB and management of tenant-based irrigation schemes (Encyclopedia of Earth. "Water Profile of Kenya," 2008). A national irrigation policy and legal framework is being developed to coordinate and regulate the irrigation sub-sector. Before a comprehensive irrigation policy is fully implemented, the operation and management of smallholder irrigation schemes are being supervised by the guidelines developed by the Ministry of Agriculture, and the Ministry of Water Resources Management and Development.

In Kenya, the other water problem is related to the conflicting water needs among different development programs, especially between agriculture and wildlife preservation. Wildlife often exists in areas where irrigation schemes take place. To address this issue, the National Environmental Management and Coordinating Act (EMCA) No.8 of 1999 allows the government to assess the environmental impact of development and through the establishment of National Environment Management Authority (NEMA) to enforce it. According to this act, an environmental impact assessment is mandatory before the implementation of a project such as large-scale agriculture, use of pesticides, introduction of new animals and plants, use of fertilizers and irrigation development.

As mentioned earlier, in the United States and in Latin America, a similar conflict about different water needs exists between the agricultural sector and other economic activities, especially mining.

Conclusion

The aforementioned discussions demonstrate that like food and energy, water insecurity derives from an ill conceived development model. For a long time, we lack a long-term and comprehensive thinking on global sustainable development. We have allowed the "winnership" model to prevail in global development. This model is based on a "zero-sum game" mentality that pursues unlimited and unselected consumption as the key driver for economic growth at the cost of our environment. And this economic growth, as measured by GDP indicators, is equated with development. So far, this model has generated a few benefits but is overshadowed by even larger disadvantages and perils that are threatening the future of humanity in a significant way.

It is true that the conventional growth model has advanced new frontiers of innovations and discoveries, especially in technologies and medicine, but few of those have been translated into equalizing the inequities on a massive scale. The financial crisis that started in 2008 was not an accident but the inevitable consequence of unlimited growth at all cost. The cost is immense, and now it is now obvious that we are paying for the cost of depletion of natural resources; environmental degradation and pollution; enlarging inequities in almost every sphere of global lives, especially in access to water, food, health, wealth, and education; and ceaseless inter-group conflicts.

Yet the worst result of this growth model is that ultra materialism and "do-it-at-all-cost profiteering" has created disconnect among humanity and led to dwindling of the community capital, the glue that binds humanity. In the framework of the growth model, anything goes in the pursuit of profit and growth. This leads to the prevalence of "not-in-my-backyard-ism," "environmental imperialism" and "hit-and-run" profiteering. Examples abound about how these forms of thinking manifest themselves in large or small scales. It is acceptable to ship the environmental waste or polluting industries to developing countries or poorer neighborhoods in developed countries as long as it is not in "my neighborhood" or "my backyard." It is acceptable to wage a war on other territories as long as it is not on my turf. It is acceptable that one takes all the profit by any means as long as other people suffer the loss of jobs or cannot afford to pay their mortgage. It is acceptable that others do not have health care coverage as long as I have it. It is acceptable to pollute the farm land in the name of GDP growth. It is acceptable to dump the pollutants in the rivers as long as I am drinking the purified water. The community capital in the form of solidarity mechanisms is rapidly diminishing while ultra-materialism and profiteering is expanding at every front of social lives.

Global development does not have to go in that direction of the "doomsday scenario." When it comes to the solutions, we actually have choices. We can continue the old way of thinking and face grave consequences. Or we can start by following a different path of development.

The global financial crisis in 2008 has shown there are serious conceptual as well as operational problems in the "winnership" development model. The fact that this model of economic growth generates more negatives than positives makes the growth "superficial" and not sustainable.

It is obvious that the winnership model has fueled the irrational growth in global consumption, which has created a very large wealth gap. The fast and large concentration of wealth in a few hands creates an even higher demand for risky, high-return investments. This demand has led to the generation of risky financial products to meet this insatiable appetite for higher profit rates among the haves. For the haves, the insatiable appetite has also led to the competition for the natural resources, especially bio-fuels, to keep the economic growth game going. The means of competition range from the metaphysical, such as ideological confrontation or cultural imperialism, to the physical, i.e., conflicts and wars. The have-nots are more and more marginalized in this global game in terms of their access to resources to meet basic needs, which creates an even more risky condition for the occurrence of diseases, inter-group rivalry, land disputes, and plundering of the natural environment. Consequently, problems multiply and fester each other.

It is obvious the model does not work well for the long-term development of humanity. Since the end of the Cold War in late 1980s, global events have shown that humanity shares a common manifest destiny and shares a real common interest, i.e., our long-term survival. Our enemy is no longer the other state, the other civilization, or the other bloc of alliance. It is our collective failure to support other human beings and protect our ecosystem. If there's anything positive about these challenging events facing humanity is that we have learned that just like global epidemics, ill thought-out development plans do not discriminate in the consequences that they generate. The most dreadful enemy of humanity is not a state or a certain group but the failure of short-sighted plans that give rise to other common threats. For example, unselected growth strategy gives rise to the green house effects. The greenhouse effects then give rise to global warming, which in turn gives rise to climate change. Then, climate changes bring about large-impact disasters, and food and water insecurity, which then leads to global economic instability, and this chain of events can go on and on.

For a long time, it was believed that the "epidemic" of underdevelopment was solely the problems facing certain states or communities, such as those in Africa, Latin America or Asia, dictated by certain social or historical conditions. "Developed" countries are immune from this epidemic. Yet the global financial crisis in 2008 shows that the world is interconnected in terms of the sharing of problems as well as the solutions for problems.

The starting point to correct these problems is to recognize that we need a radical departure to conceptualize the growth of humanity and that we need a totally different operational model to resolve the past mistakes in development. The proposed inclusive sustainable development theory aims for such a departure.

The inclusive sustainable development theory proposed in this book applies a post-ideological approach in the conceptualization of development. That is, we need a community-centered, equitable, and balanced growth approach in how we think of human development. It means that we will have to reverse most of the assumptions about global development in the "winnership" model that pits one state against the other; that see gains of one power as a loss for the others; and the self-interest of a given state or an alliance is incompatible with those of the other groups, communities, or other states.

The inclusive sustainable development theory is designed to be the theoretical and operational opposite of the winnership model by emphasizing equitable, balanced growth of humanity, aiming for re-generation and multiplication of the gains of development programs in the context of interdependence and collaboration. In practice, the Hexagon of Partnership Model provides an action framework for resolving development challenges in the short term, mid term and in the long term through collaborative, multi-sector, and community-centered partnerships.

It is critical, however, that priorities are set in the right order by using this proposed theoretical framework before solutions are applied. The core issues of equity, governance, global peace, water, food and energy security, and environmental integrity have to be addressed before solutions for related problems are generated. With the right priorities and corrected path of development, these daunting challenges could become the most valuable opportunities for sustainable growth for humanity and our ecosystem.

Overall, setting priorities in the right order means that humanity needs to follow a different mindset on the future directions of development. In articulating the architecture of inclusive sustainable development theory, this book has demonstrated the goal of this new thinking should be inclusion, equity, harmony, and partnership, because in an interconnected world, misfortunes spread through a global chain. Only when our community is restored can development programs be sustainable. These ideas are not difficult to implement when the political will is in place. In facing the survival challenge, the global leadership has no other choices but to act in an inclusive partnership. That should be the "tao" of our corrected path of sustainable development.

Bibliography

Chapter 1

American Heritage Dictionary of the English Language. "Definition of Architecture."
2008. <http://education.yahoo.com/reference/dictionary/>

America's Second Harvest. "Learn about Hunger." 2008. <http://www.secondharvest.org
/learn_about_hunger/fact_sheet/poverty_stats.html>

Association of Southeast Asian Nations. (2008). "Overview." <http://www.aseansec.
org/64.htm>

AVERT. "Worldwide HIV/AIDS Statistics." 2008. <http://www.avert.org/worldstats
.htm>

BBC. "Oil Firms Discuss Iraqi Stake." 12 March, 2003. <http://news.bbc.co.uk/1/hi
/business/2842315.stm>

Benocraitis, Nijole. Subtle Sexism: Current Practice and Prospects for Change. Thousand Oaks, CA:Sage, 1997.

Cambridge Dictionaries On-line. (2008). 'Definition of Architecture.' <http://dictionary.
cambridge.org/define.asp?key=3871&dict=CALD>

Congressional Research Service. "CRS Report for Congress: Conventional Arms Transfer to Developing Nations." 2005.

Congressional Research Service. "CRS Report for Congress: <http://fpc.state.gov/ docu-
ments/organization/52179.pdf>

Crane, George T., Abla Amawi. Theoretical Evolution of International Political Economy: A Reader. New York: Oxford University, 1997.

Davies, Nicolas J. "The Crime of War:From Nuremberg to Fallujah." On-line Journal.
2004. <http://www.pegc.us/archive/Habib_v_Bush/davies_crime_of_war.pdf>

Deen, Thalif. "Climate Change:UN Brace for New Breed of Refugees." 2008.
<http://ipsnews.net/news.asp?idnews=37860>

Frank, Andre Gunder. Capitalism and Underdevelopment in Latin America. 1967. New
York: Monthly Review Press.

Genovese, Eugene D. Political Economy of Slavery: Studies in the Economy and Society
of the Slave South. New York:Vintage, 1961.

Genovese, Eugene D. The Political Economy of Slavery. New York: Vintage Books,
1967.Global Issues. "Causes of Poverty." 2008.

<http://www.globalissues.org/TradeRelated/Poverty/death/>

Global Issues. "Poverty Facts and Stats." 2008. <http://www.globalissues.org/Trade Re-
lated/Facts.asp>

Global Network of Neglected Tropical Diseases. "About Neglected Tropical Diseases."
2006. <http://gnntdc.sabin.org/what/aboutntds.html>

Harvey, David. A Brief History of Neoliberalism. Oxford: Oxford University Press, 2005.

Huntington, Samuel. The Clash of Civilization and the Remaking of World Order. New
York: Simon and Schuster, 1998.

Internationalist. "State of the World." Issue 287. February, 1997. <http://www.newint.org
/issue287/keynote.html>

Jordan, Winthrop D. (1974). *The white man's burden: Historical origins of racism in the United States.* Oxford, UK:Oxford University Press.

Kleppe, Christine. "Record Exports of Weapons." 2007. <http://www.ssb.no/english/magazine/art-2008-03-12-01-en.html>

Lobe, Jim. "Bush's Democracy Crusade Defines Public Opinion." 2005. <http://www.lewrockwell.com/ips/lobe185.html>

McClathy. "US Seeking 58 Military Bases in Iraq, Shiite Law Makers Say." <http://www.mcclatchydc.com/251/story/40372.html>

Norris, Floyd. "United Panic." The New York Times. 24 October 2008. <http://norris.blogs.nytimes.com/2008/10/24/united-panic/).

PAWSS. "Refugees, Forcible Displacement, and International security." 2008. <http://pawss.hampshire.edu/topics/refugees/index.html>

Portes, Alejandro. (1997). "Neoliberalism and the Sociology of Development:Emerging Trends and Anticipated Facts." *Population and Development Review,* 23(2): 229-59.

Prasad, Monica. *The Politics of Free Markets: The Rise of Neo-liberal Economic Policies in Britain, France, Germany and the United States.* Chicago: University of Chicago Press, 2006.

Rapley, John. *Globalization and Inequality:Neoliberalism's Downward Spiral.* Boulder, Colorado:Lynne Rienner, 2004.

Raul Prebisch. *The Economic Development of Latin America and Its Principle Problem.* New York: United Nations, 1950.

Smith, Jane Collins, Terence Hopkins, Akbar Muhammad. *Racism, Sexism and World System.* New York:Greenwood Press, 1988.

Stiglitz, Joseph. *Globalization and Its Discontents.* New York, NY: W. W. Norton and Company, 2003.

Twells, Alison and Christine Smith. *Colonialism, Slavery and Industrial Revolution: A Case Study, the Empire in South Yorkshore, C. 1700-1860.* South Yorkshore, UK: Development Education Center, 1992.

United Nations Development Program. "Human Development Report 1998." 1998. <http://hdr.undp.org/en/reports/global/hdr1998/>

United Nations Development Program. "Human Development Program 1999." 1999. <http://hdr.undp.org/en/reports/global/hdr1999/>

United Nations. "Millennium Development Goals Report 2007. <http://www. globalissues.org/TradeRelated/Facts.asp>

UNICEFF."The State of the World's Children." 1999.<http://www.unicef.org/sowc99/index.html>

United Nations Human Development Program. "Human Development Report 2006." 2006. <http://hdr.undp.org/en/reports/global/hdr2006/>

United Nations Development Program. (2007). "Human Development Report 2007." <http://www.globalissues.org/TradeRelated/Facts.asp#src9>

United Nations Development Program. 2008. "Armed Violence in Africa:Reflections on the Costs of Crime and Conflict." 2008. <http://www.genevadeclaration.org/pdfs/crime_and_conflict.pdf>

United Nations. "Water: A Matter of Life and Death." 2003. <http://www.un.org/events/water/factsheet.pdf>

White House. "President's Remarks at the United Nations General Assembly." 2002. <http://www.whitehouse.gov/news/releases/2002/09/20020912-1.html>

Wikipedia. "2003 Invasion of Iraq." <http://en.wikipedia.org/wiki/2003_invasion_of_Iraq>

Wikipedia "Financial Cost of the Iraq War." 2008. <http://en.wikipedia.org/wiki /Financial_cost_of_the_Iraq_War#cite_note-0>

Wikipedia. National Priorities Project. 2008. <http://www.nationalpriorities.org/ costof-war_home>

Wikipedia. "Financial Cost of Iraq War." 2008. <http://en.wikipedia.org/wiki/Financial_ cost_of_the_Iraq_War#cite_note-0>

Wisebrot, Mark, Dean Baker, Egor Kraef, and Judy Chen. "The Scorecard of Globalization 1980-2000: Twenty Years' Diminished Progress." Center of Economic Policy and Research. 2001. <http://www.cepr.net/globalization/scorecard_on_globalization .htm>

World Bank. "Key Development Data and Statistics." <http://web.worldbank.org /WBSITE/EXTERNAL/DATASTATISTICS/0,,contentMDK:20535285~menuPK:1 192694~pagePK:64133150~piPK:64133175~theSitePK:239419,00.html>

World Health Organization. (2008). "Malaria." <http://www.who.int/mediacentre /factsheets/fs094/en/index.html>

World Health Organization. "Control of Neglected Tropical Diseases." 2008. <http://www.who.int/neglected_diseases/en/>

World Hunger Education Service. "World Hunger Facts 2008." 2008. <http://www. worldhunger.org/articles/Learn/world%20hunger%20facts%202002.htm>

Yahoo News. (October, 2008). "Retirement accounts have lost $2 trillion so far." <http://news.yahoo.com/s/ap/20081007/ap_on_bi_ge/meltdown_retirement>

Chapter 2

Baby Milk Action. "Update." 22 June, 1998. <http://www.babymilkaction.org /update/update22.html>

Centers of Disease Control and Prevention. "Recent Trends in Infant Mortality in the United States." NCHS Data Brief, Number 9, October 2008. <http://www.cdc.gov/nchs/data/databriefs/db09.htm>

Daniels, Norman, Bruce Kennedy and Ichiro Kawachi. "Justice Is Good for Our Health." Boston Review, February/March, 2000. <http://www.bostonreview.net/BR25.1 /daniels.html>

Diamond, Jared. Guns, Germs, and Steel: The Fates of Human Societies. New York: Random House, 1997.

Eghbal, Media. "BRIC Economies Withstand Global Financial Crisis." Euromonitor (November 5, 2008). <http://www.euromonitor.com/Articles.aspx?folder=BRIC_ economies_withstand_global_financial_crisis&print=true>

Financial Times. "Food Crisis is a Chance to Reform Global Agriculture." 30 April 30, 2008. <http://blogs.ft.com/wolfforum/2008/04/food-crisis-is-a-chance-to-reform-global-agriculture/>

Global Issues. "Global Food Crisis 2008." 2008. <http://www.globalissues.org/ food/crisis-2008>

Hurst, Charles E. "Social Inequality: Forms, Causes, and Consequences." Pearson Education, Inc., 2007.

Holt-Giménez, Eric and Peabody, Loren. "From Food Rebellions to Food Sovereignty: Urgent Call to Fix a Broken Food System." 16 May, 2008. <http://www.foodfirst. org/en/node/2120>

Intergovernmental Panel on Climate Change. "Climate Change 2001: The Scientific Basis." 2001. <http://www.grida.no/climate/ipcc_tar/wg1/index.htm>

International Encyclopedia of Communication. 2008. <http://www.blackwellreference
.com/public/tocnode?id=g9781405131995_chunk_g978140513199510_ss24-1>

Interview with Felipa, Director of Mujeres en Action. 14 January, 2007. Los Angeles
Times. "Midwest Floods' Economic Fallout Uncertain." (22 June, 2008).
<http://www.latimes.com/news/nationworld/nation/la-na-floodtoll22-2008jun22,0
,525636.story>

Macrohistory and World Report. The Iranian Revolution. <http://www.fsmitha.com/h2/
ch29ir.html> 2007

National Public Radio. "Income Disparity Persists Between Blacks, Whites." 14 November, 2007. <http://www.npr.org/templates/story/story.php?storyId=16293332>

Nature. "Global Water Crisis." 2008. <http://www.nature.com/nature/focus/water/>

Oppenheimer, Stephen. "Out of Africa: Human Roots." Prospect, No. 91 October 2003.
<http://www.prospect-magazine.co.uk/article_details.php?id=5732.>

Pathfinder. "Social Stratification in the United States." 2008. <http://www.ils
.unc.edu/dpr/path/socialstrat/>

People's Daily. "Economic Globalization Widens Wealth Gap: UN Official." (9 June,
2001). <http://www.mindfully.org/WTO/Wealth-Gap-UN9jun01.htm>

Perlmutter, Howard. "Deep Dialogue." 2006. <http://www.deepdialog.com/dr_ perlmut-
ter/articles.html>

RALPH (The Review of Arts, Literature, Philosophy and the Humanities). "Breast vs.
Bottle, Part I." (Early Winter, 2003-2004). No.107. <http://www.ralphmag.org/CK/
1breast-vs-bottle.html>

Reuters. "U.S. Midwest farmland flooding boosts food prices." 17 June, 2008.
<http://www.reuters.com/article/latestCrisis/idUSN17360927>

Russell, Gold and Ann Davis, "Oil Officials See Limit Looming on Production." The
Wall Street Journal. November 10, 2007. <http://www.theoildrum.com/node/3265>

Thorpe, Jacqueline. "Chinese Dragon to fire up G20 Meeting." Financial Post.
(13 November, 2008). <http://www.financialpost.com/most_popular/story.html?id=
956352>

UNESCO. "CUBES and Spheres." 2002. <http://portal.unesco.org/en/ev.php-
URL_ID=6686&URL_DO=DO_TOPIC&URL_SECTION=201.html>

United Nations. "Report of the World Commission on Environment and Development."
General Assembly Resolution 42/187, 11 December 1987.

US Census Bureau. "World Population Information." June 24, 2008. <http://www.
census.gov/ipc/www/idb/worldpopinfo.html>

Wang, Mei-ling. Global Health Partnerships: Pharmaceutical Industry and BRICAs. Lon-
don, UK: Palgrave MacMillan, 2008.

Wang, Mei-ling. "Toward a New Theory of Social Exclusion, Community Capital. and
Global Health." Unpublished Paper Reported at Intercultural Communication
Course. 27 January, 2005. University of the Sciences in Philadelphia.

Wang, Mei-ling and Nantulya, Vinand. Social Exclusion and Community Capital: The
Missing Link in Global Partnerships of Health for All. 2008. Lanham, MD:
University Press of America.

Washington Post. "He's The Worst Ever." 3 December, 2006. <http://www.washington
ost.com/wp-dyn/content/article/2006/12/01/AR2006120101509.html>

Wikipedia. "Community.". <http://en.wikipedia.org/wiki/Community>

Wikipedia, "History of Agriculture," 2008. <http://en.wikipedia.org/wiki/istory_of_
griculture>

Wikipedia (2008). "Iranian Revolution." <http://en.wikipedia.org/wiki/Iranian_ Rvolu-
tion>

Wikipedia, "Recent African origin of modern humans. 2008. <http://en.wikipedia.org/ wiki/single-origin_hypothesis>
Wikipedia. "2007–2008 world food price crisis." <http://en.wikipedia.org/wiki/ Food_crisis>
World Bank. "Food Price Crisis Imperils 100 Million in Poor Countries, Zoellick Says." The World Bank News & Broadcast. 14 April, 2008
Worldometers. " Current World Population." 24 June, 2008, <http://www.worldometers .info/population/>

Chapter 3

Barron's. "Update: Solar Stocks Rally On China Subsidy Plan." (March 26, 2009). http://blogs.barrons.com/techtraderdaily/2009/03/26/update-solar-stocks-rally-on-china-subsidy-plan/).
Burgermeister, Jane. "Germany: The World's First Major Renewable Energy Economy." April 3, 2009. Renewable Energy World.Com. <http://www.renewableenergyworld .com/rea/news/article/2009/04/germany-the-worlds-first-major-renewable-energy-economy?src=rss>
Economist. "Cheap No More." December 6, 2007. <http://www.economist.com/ display-story.cfm?story_id=10250420>
Environment Leader. "U.S. Now Largest Producer of Wind Energy." February 5, 2009. <http://www.environmentalleader.com/2009/02/05/us-now-largest-producer-of-wind -energy/>
Fialka, John J. "Search for Crude Comes With New Dangers," *Wall Street Journal*, *April 11*, 2005
Food and Agriculture Organization. 'Food Outlook." November, 2008. <http://www.fao.org/docrep/011/ai474e/ai474e00.htm>
Food and Agriculture Organization. 'Clinton at UN: food, energy, financial woes linked.' (October 24, 2008). <http://www.fao.org/newsroom/en/news/2008/1000945 /index.html>
Food and Agricultural Organization.. "Special Report: Crop and Food Supply Situation in Kenya. July 10, 2000. <http://www.fao.org/DOCREP/004/X7697E/X7697E00 .HTM>
Food and Agricultural Organization (FAO). "World Food Summit." <http://www.fao.org/ docrep/003/w3613e/w3613e00.HTM>
Global Monitoring for Food Security. (2007). "Food Security." <http://esamultimedia.esa.int/docs/GMES/Info_Day/consortia/5_infod_GMFS_over view_8_03_07_v3.pdf>
IRIN. "Kenya. It's the Economy, Stupid." January 9, 2008. <http://www.irinnews. org/Report.aspx?ReportId=76159>
Kenya Food Security Meeting. "Food Security in Kenya." 2008. <http://www.kenya foodsecurity.org/index.php>
Kenya Food Security. "KFSSG's LONG RAINS ASSESSMENT REPORT, 2008." 2008. <http://www.kenyafoodsecurity.org/longrains08/consolidated_lra_report.pdf>
Klare, Michael T. "Global Struggle for Energy." Mother Jones Journal (May 9, 2005). <http://www.motherjones.com/news/dailymojo/2005/05/energy.html>
Reuters. "Post-election conflict causes extreme food insecurity in rural areas, urban centers." January 2008. <http://www.alertnet.org/thenews /newsdesk/FEWS /cfc49b84 a576caecabc88300f6828aed.htm>

Stimson Center. "US TRAINING, AFRICAN PEACEKEEPING: The Global Peace Operations Initiative (GPOI)." July 2007. <http://www.stimson.org/fopo/pdf/ Stimson_GPOIBrief_Aug07.pdf>

The Christian Science Monitor. "Out of Kenya's violence, rebirth." February 12, 2008. <http://www.csmonitor.com/2008/0212/p09s02-coop.html>

The Economic Times. "Now, EU Says Increased Meat Consumption in India, China Driving Food Prices." May 6, 2008. . <http://economictimes.indiatimes.com/Now_EU_says_increased_meat_consumption_in_India_driving_food_prices_/articleshow/3016503.cms>

The National Council of NGOs. "NGO Support Organizations." 2003. <http://www.ngocouncil.org/support.asp>

United Nations. UN Department of Economic and Social Affairs. January 2008. <http://www.un.org/esa/sustdev/documents/agreed.htm>

Washington Post. "Global Food Crisis." 26 April, 2008. . <http://www. washingtonpost.com/wp-dyn/content/article/2008/04/26/AR2008042601723.html>   or <http://www.washingtonpost.com/wp-srv/world/globalfoodcrisis/>

Washington Post. "The New Economics of Hunger." April 27, 2008 <http://www. washingtonpost.com/wp-dyn/content/story/2008/04/26/ST2008042602333.html>

White,Todd and Rachel Graham. "U.S. Takes Global Lead in Wind Power, Passes Germany." 2 February, 2009. Bloomberg News. <http://www.bloomberg.com/apps/news?pid=20601100&sid=a5qyeN9A6LlY&refer=germany>

Wikipedia. "2007–2008 world food price crisis." . <http://en.wikipedia.org/wiki/Food_crisis>

Chapter 4

Acreman, Mike. "Water and Ethics: Water and Ecology." Water and Ethics Essay 8. UNESCO. <http://unesdoc.unesco.org/images/0013/001363/136355e.pdf>

Asia News Net. "Sixty Thousand People Protest Against Pollution." 15 April, 2005. <http://www.asianews.it/index.php?art=3036&l=en>.

Ayibotele, N.B. The World's Water: Assessing the Resource. Keynote Paper at the International Conference on Water and Environment: Development issues for the 21st Century, January 26-31, 1992. Dublin, Ireland.

BBC. "'No water' in cholera-hit Harare." (1 December, 2008). <http://news.bbc.co.uk/2/hi/africa/7758147.stm>

Burton, Lloyd. *American Indian Water Rights and the Limits of Law.* Kansas City, Kansas: University of Kansas Press, 1991.

Commonwealth Parliamentary Conference. "Access to Water in Developing Countries." Commonwealth Parliamentary Conference, India, 2007. <http://www.cpahq.org/ uploadedFiles/Programmes_and_Activities/Professional_Development/DP%203. DOC>

Encyclopedia Britannica. "Monsoon." 2009. <http://www.britannica.com/EBchecked/topic/390302/monsoon>

Encyclopedia of Earth. "Water Profile of Kenya." 2008. <http://www.eoearth.org/article/Water_profile_of_Kenya>

Gleick, Peter. "The World's Water, 2008-2009: Chapter 5, China and Water. 2009. <http://www.worldwater.org/data20082009/ch05.pdf>

González, Gustavo. Environment: Chile Gold Mining Project Threatens Andean Gla-
    ciers." 2005. <http://ipsnews.net/news.asp?idnews=29223>

Greenpeace. "Water Pollution Has Become China's Most Urgent Environmental Problem
    Today." 2008. <http://www.greenpeace.org/china/en/campaigns/toxics/water-
    pollution>

Guardian. "The problem of mining in the Andes? You have to move glaciers." 3 May,
    2006. <http://www.guardian.co.uk/business/2006/may/03/businesscomment.chile>

HARC. "The Role of Fresh Water Inflows in Sustaining Estuarine Ecosystem Health in
    San Antonio Bay Region." 15 September, 2006. <http://files.harc.edu
    /Projects/Nature/SanAntonioFreshwaterInflows.pdf>

Hinrichsen, Don. "Fresh Water: Lifeblood of the Planet." (2008). People and Planet Net.
    <http://www.peopleandplanet.net/doc.php?id=671&section=14>

Info For Health. "Consequences of Overuse and Pollution." 1998. <http://www. infofor-
    health.org/pr/m14/m14chap4.shtml>

Info For Health. "The Coming Era of Water Stress and Scarcity." 1998. <http://www.
    infoforhealth.org/pr/m14/m14chap3_2.shtml>

International Relations and Security Network (IRIN). "A Thirsty World." 2009. <
    <http://www.isn.ethz.ch/isn/Current-Affairs/Special-Reports/A-Thirsty-World/
    Backgrounder/>

Kusler, Jon A. "Definitions of the Terms Wetland 'Function' and 'Value.'" Association
    of State Wetland Managers. <http://www.aswm.org/propub/16_functions_6_
    26_06.pdf>

Mason, Margie. "Drugs in the Water ; Pharmaceutical Contamination of Water is an
    Emerging Concern Worldwide, With India Showing the Highest Concentrations."
    25 January, 2009. <http://www.americanchronicle.com/articles/yb/125760099>

NPR. "Zimbabwe Cholera Tied To Crumbling Infrastructure." <http://www.npr.org/
    templates/story/story.php?storyId=98348270>

Oliver, Rachel. "All about Water and Health." For CNN. 18 December, 2007.
    http://www.hvr.se/pdf/All%20About%20Water%20and%20Health.pdf>

Pacific Environment. "China Program." 2008. <http://www.pacificenvironment.
    rg/article.php?id=1878>

Pacific Environment. "Water Pollution in China." 2009. < <http://www.pacific environ-
    ment.org/article.php?id=1878>

Public Employees for Environmental Responsibility (PEER). "Testimony for May 13,
    2008 Oversight Hearing on Reports of Pharmaceutical Contamination in Public Wa-
    ter Supplies." 2008. <http://www.peer.org/docs/ma/08_12_5_ppcp_testimony.pdf>

RAMSAR. "Economic Valuation of Wetlands: an Important Component of Wetland
    Management Strategies at the River Basin Scale." May 2003.
    <://www.ramsar.org/features/features_econ_val1.htm>

Rosengrant, M. W. "Dealing with Water Scarcity in the Next Century." 2020 Vision
    Brief 21. Washington DC: International Food Policy Research Institute, 1995.
    <http://www.ifpri.org/2020/BRIEFS/NUMBER21.HTM>

Spiegel Online. "Choking on Pollution in India." July 2007. <
    <http://www.spiegel.de/international/world/0,1518,493033,00.html>

Sustainability. "Unstable ecosystems challenge society." Issue 1 (January 2009).
    <http://sustainability.formas.se/en/Issues/Issue-1-Januari-2009/Content/Articles
    /Unstable-ecosystems-challenge-society/>

UNESCO. "One Size does not Fit All." Natural Science Quarterly Newsletter 6, no. 4
    (October-December, 2008). <http://www.unesco.org/science/document/AWOS_
    Vol6_4web.pdf>

United   Nations   Development   Programme.   "Action   on   Water."   2006.
    <http://hdr.undp.org/en/media/HDR_2006_Presskit_EN.pdf>
United Nations Economic and Social Council. COMMISSION ON HUMAN RIGHTS
    Sub-Commission on Prevention of Discrimination and Protection of Minorities
    Working Group on Indigenous Populations. E/CN.4/Sub.2/AC.4/1996/3/Add.1 GE.
    96-16746 (E). 12 June, 1996. http://www.cwis.org/fwdp/Americas/96-16746.txt
United Nations Environment Programme. "Fresh Water Under Threat: South Asia. 2008.
    <http://www.unep.org/pdf/southasia_report.pdf>
Voice of America. "Zimbabwe Cholera Crisis Mounts As Harare Water System Shut
    Down." 1 December, 2008. <http://www.voanews.com/english/archive/2008-
    12/2008-12-01-voa65.cfm?CFID=117743446&CFTOKEN=14797525&jsessionid
    =00302c943b95c4f459d6583644a4612346a4>
Water Is Life. "Water Wars and International Conflict." 2004. <http://academic
    .evergreen.edu/g/grossmaz/OFORIAA/>
Webb, Patrick and Maria Iskandarani. "Water Insecurity and the Poor: Issues and Re-
    search Needs." Discussion Papers on Development Policy: No. 2. 1998.
    <http://www.zef.de/fileadmin/webfiles/downloads/zef_dp/zef_dp2-98.pdf>
Wikinvest. "China's Water Scarcity." 2009. <http://www.wikinvest.com/concept/
    China's_Water_Scarcity>
Wikipedia. "China Water Crisis." Wikipedia. 2009. <http://en.wikipedia.org/wiki/China
    _water_crisis>
Wikipedia. "Ministry of Water Resources of the People's Republic of China." 2008.
    <http://en.wikipedia.org/wiki/Ministry_of_Water_Resources_of_the_People's_Repu
    blic_of_China>
Wikipedia. "Water Pollution." 2008. <http://en.wikipedia.org/wiki/Water_pollution>
Water Is Life. "Water Wars and International Conflict." 2004. <http://academic. ever-
    green.edu/g/grossmaz/OFORIAA/>
World Resource. "Will There be Enough Water?" 2007. <http://earthtrends.wri.
    org/features/view_feature.php?theme=1&fid=17>
World Water Council. "Water Supply and Sanitation. 2008. <http://worldwaterforum5
    .org/index.php?id=23>
World Watch Institute. "Fresh Water Species at Increasing Risk." <http://uregina.ca/~
    piwowarj/geog326/Freshwater%20Species%20at%20Risk.pdf>
WWF International. "World's Top 10 Rivers at Risk." March, 2007.
    <http://assets.panda.org/downloads/worldstop10riversatriskfinalmarch13.pdf>

About the Author

Mei-ling Wang

Dr. Mei-ling Wang, graduate of Harvard School of Public Health, is professor, researcher, writer, and global development partnership theorist. She has focused on global health, sustainable development challenges, and partnership building in most of her writings, including the following books: *The Dust that Never Settles*; *WTO, Globalization, and China's Health Care System*; *Global Health Partnerships: Pharmaceutical Industry and BRIC*; and *Social Exclusion and Community Capital: The Missing Link in Global Partnerships of Health for All*. In addition, she has made more than 70 presentations in national and global meetings. In her writings, she has linked global health and development challenges to broader contextual factors, such as peace-building, policy and governance, social and cultural practices, and macro-economic changes. Among the various solutions offered in her writings, global inclusive dialogue and partnerships are deemed as the most important.

In addition to her academic work, she is also a practitioner in global health and development. She is advocate for the excluded populations in her field work. For example, she co-directed the Social Exclusion Knowledge Network for the World Health Organization. She has also founded the Global Health and Sustainable Development Partnerships group to work on development projects for the vulnerable people. She can be contacted at: globalpartnership@ymail.com.

www.ingramcontent.com/pod-product-compliance
Lightning Source LLC
Chambersburg PA
CBHW021823270326
41932CB00007B/308